D1115070

John Wiley & Sons, Inc.

111 River St.
Hoboken, NJ 07030-5774

ISBN 978-1-118-04596-1 (paper); ISBN 978-1-118-12788-9 (ebk);
ISBN 978-1-118-12789-6 (ebk); ISBN 978-1-118-12790-2 (ebk)

Editor: Jennifer Reilly
Production Editor: Erin Amick
Photo Editor: Richard Fox
Cartographer: Roberta Stockwell
Production by Wiley Indianapolis Composition Services

For information on our other products and services or to obtain technical
support, please contact our Customer Care Department within the U.S.
at 877/762-2974, outside the U.S. at 317/572-3993 or fax 317/572-4002.

Wiley also publishes its books in a variety of electronic formats. Some
content that appears in print may not be available in electronic formats.

Manufactured in China

5   4   3   2   1

A Note from the Editorial Director

Organizing your time. That's what this guide is all about.

Other guides give you long lists of things to see and do and then expect you to fit the pieces together. The Day by Day guides are different. These guides tell you the best of everything, and then they show you how to see it in the *smartest, most time-efficient way*. Our authors have designed detailed itineraries organized by time, neighborhood, or special interest. And each tour comes with a bulleted map that takes you from stop to stop.

Hoping to see the best museums in Athens or stroll around the Acropolis? Planning a walk through Syntagma Square, or plotting a day in the Greek islands? Whatever your interest or schedule, the Day by Days give you the smartest routes to follow. Not only do we take you to the top attractions, hotels, and restaurants, but we also help you access those special moments that locals get to experience—those "finds" that turn tourists into travelers.

The Day by Days are also your top choice if you're looking for one complete guide for all your travel needs. The best hotels and restaurants for every budget, the greatest shopping values, the wildest nightlife—it's all here.

Why should you trust our judgment? Because our authors personally visit each place they write about. They're an independent lot who say what they think and would never include places they wouldn't recommend to their best friends. They're also open to suggestions from readers. If you'd like to contact them, please send your comments our way at feedback@frommers.com, and we'll pass them on.

Enjoy your Day by Day guide—the most helpful travel companion you can buy. And have the trip of a lifetime.

Warm regards,

Kelly Regan

Kelly Regan, Editorial Director
Frommer's Travel Guides

About the Author

Stephen Brewer is a writer and editor who has worked in magazines, books, radio, and corporate communications for more than 30 years. He visited Athens 20 years ago, decided he found his place in the world, and has spent part of each year in the city ever since. He is also a co-author of *Frommer's Greece Day by Day*.

Advisory & Disclaimer

Travel information can change quickly and unexpectedly, and we strongly advise you to confirm important details locally before traveling, including information on visas, health and safety, traffic and transport, accommodations, shopping, and eating out. We also encourage you to stay alert while traveling and to remain aware of your surroundings. Avoid civil disturbances, and keep a close eye on cameras, purses, wallets, and other valuables.

While we have endeavored to ensure that the information contained within this guide is accurate and up-to-date at the time of publication, we make no representations or warranties with respect to the accuracy or completeness of the contents of this work and specifically disclaim all warranties, including without limitation warranties of fitness for a particular purpose. We accept no responsibility or liability for any inaccuracy or errors or omissions, or for any inconvenience, loss, damage, costs, or expenses of any nature whatsoever incurred or suffered by anyone as a result of any advice or information contained in this guide.

The inclusion of a company, organization, or website in this guide as a service provider and/or potential source of further information does not mean that we endorse them or the information they provide. Be aware that information provided through some websites may be unreliable and can change without notice. Neither the publisher nor author shall be liable for any damages arising herefrom.

Star Ratings, Icons & Abbreviations

Every hotel, restaurant, and attraction listing in this guide has been ranked for quality, value, service, amenities, and special features using a star-rating system. Hotels, restaurants, attractions, shopping, and nightlife are rated on a scale of zero stars (recommended) to three stars (exceptional). In addition to the star-rating system, we also use a **kids** icon to point out the best bets for families. Within each tour, we recommend cafes, bars, or restaurants where you can take a break. Each of these stops appears in a shaded box marked with a coffee-cup-shaped bullet ☕.

The following **abbreviations** are used for credit cards:

AE	American Express	DISC	Discover	V	Visa
DC	Diners Club	MC	MasterCard		

Travel Resources at Frommers.com

Frommer's travel resources don't end with this guide. Frommer's website, **www.frommers.com,** has travel information on more than 4,000 destinations. We update features regularly, giving you access to the most current trip-planning information and the best airfare, lodging, and car-rental bargains. You can also listen to podcasts, connect with other Frommers.com members through our active-reader forums, share your travel photos, read blogs from guidebook editors and fellow travelers, and much more.

A Note on Prices

In the "Take a Break" and "Best Bets" sections of this book, we have used a system of dollar signs to show a range of costs for 1 night in a hotel (the price of a double-occupancy room) or the cost of an entree at a restaurant. Use the following table to decipher the dollar signs:

Cost	Hotels	Restaurants
$	under 100€	under 10€
$$	100€–200€	10€–20€
$$$	200€–300€	20€–30€
$$$$	300€–400€	30€–40€
$$$$$	over 400€	over 40€

An Invitation to the Reader

In researching this book, we discovered many wonderful places—hotels, restaurants, shops, and more. We're sure you'll find others. Please tell us about them, so we can share the information with your fellow travelers in upcoming editions. If you were disappointed with a recommendation, we'd love to know that, too. Please write to:

Frommer's Athens Day by Day, 2nd Edition
John Wiley & Sons, Inc. • 111 River St. • Hoboken, NJ 07030-5774

15 Favorite
Moments

15 Favorite **Moments**

Previous page: When floodlit at night, the Acropolis is visible from almost every corner of A

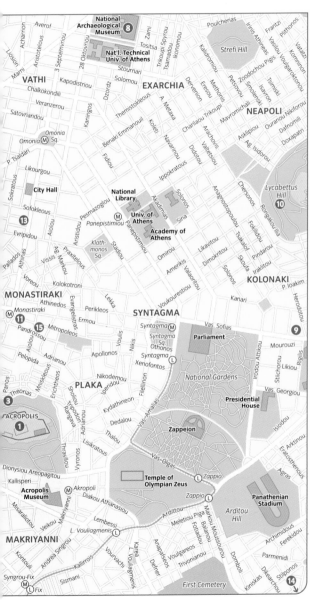

The wonders of Athens go beyond the Parthenon, hard as it is to match that most exquisite landmark. Much of the fun is just wandering the streets of this anarchic, free-wheeling city that extends a warm welcome to its endless stream of visitors. Take in the great treasures of antiquity, soak in some street life, enjoy a meal outdoors—here are some of the many ways to enjoy the capital.

Dining under the Acropolis in the Plaka district.

1 Gazing at the Acropolis. You don't have to go out of your way to find a vantage point. The best approach is to let the sight take you unaware—let it catch you by surprise as you look up from a narrow side street or traffic-choked square. In fact, the more mundane the surroundings from which you catch a glimpse of the Acropolis, the more remarkable this ancient wonder seems. At night, the floodlit ruins on Acropolis Hill are especially spectacular. *See p 9.*

2 Having a meal on the terrace of a taverna. Almost any taverna will do. The food at most is usually pretty good, and often great, and it's all about the experience. You'll be made to feel right at home (a cat or two might rub against your legs), and watching the city passing by is like being in the theater. *See p 98.*

3 Wandering into Anafiotika. My favorite Athens neighborhood is not posh or trendy. Transporting is the word. The lower slopes of the Acropolis just above the Plaka were settled by craftsmen from the island of Anafi who came to Athens in the mid–19th century to work on the new buildings transforming the capital; they recreated their homeland with stepped streets and white cubical houses. Blue shutters, balconies with bougainvillea cascading over the railings, little blue domed chapels, the works—you'll feel like you've been whisked off to a Cycladic island. *See p 62.*

4 Envisioning life as it once was in the Agora. Athens has no shortage of ancient ruins, but those of the Agora, the marketplace and social center of the ancient city, are the most evocative. Most of the shops and stoas have been reduced to rubble, but just enough remains (including the best-preserved Greek temple in the world and an ancient clock tower and weather station) to give you an idea of what the place must have been like when Socrates sat with his students on shady porticos and vendors hawked spices and oils. *See p 9.*

5 **Seeing the reliefs in the Acropolis Museum.** More than any other ancient pieces, these fragments of exquisitely carved marble capture snippets of good-natured divinity and humanity—in one, the goddess Athena Nike fastens her sandal (something you didn't think goddesses had to do); priests, soldiers, and ordinary citizens parade across the Parthenon friezes, and you almost want to jump in and join the procession. *See p 28.*

6 **Experiencing an outdoor theater.** A bit like an American drive-in, with a distinctly Athenian twist: The Cine Paris and other **open-air, rooftop cinemas** screen films under the stars, accompanied by a breeze, a glass of wine, and in some cases an Acropolis view. For live action, take a seat in the **Odeon of Herodes Atticus** for classical drama or opera. *See p 128.*

7 **Walking along the Grand Promenade.** Even Athenians get a thrill every time they follow this walkway around the base of the Acropolis Hill past some of the

greatest monuments of antiquity. Think of the experience as time travel. *See p 26.*

8 **Getting lost in the National Archaeological Museum for a couple of hours.** You don't have to be a classics scholar to realize you've stumbled into an embarrassment of riches at Athens archaeology museum. No need to be methodical in your approach, just wander and stop in front of the pieces that catch your eye: All those figures frozen in marble for eternity; all that gold, jewelry, and pottery. My favorites are the colorful frescoes that capture residents of the Minoan settlement of Akrotiri on Santorini going about everyday life as it was more than 3,500 years ago. *See p 38.*

9 **Admiring the figures in the Museum of Cycladic Art.** It's hard to distinguish the smooth, oblong, elongated figures from the modern pieces of Henry Moore, Picasso, and Modigliani they've inspired. Their timelessness is haunting. *See p 14.*

10 **Seeing Athens from the top of Mount Lycabettus.** Of the many heights in the city, this craggy, pine-covered rise—Athens's highest hill—provides the best vantage point. You don't have to be a kid to think the ride up on the Teleferik (funicular) is

Athens's Agora.

a heck of a lot of fun, and the walk back down into Kolonaki is invigorating. You'll surely get a kick out of being so high above Athens, catching the breeze, and seeing the spectacle of the city spreading out at your feet and the Aegean glistening in the distance. *See p 87.*

⑪ Eating souvlaki on "Kebab Street." Head to the bottom of Mitropoleos Street in Monastaraki and take a whiff—a dozen or so tavernas serve deliciously juicy lamb. Sit down at one of the outdoor tables for a full meal or a skewer, washed down with a cold beer. How much better can a casual meal be? *See p 105.*

⑫ Sailing from Piraeus. Where else could you take a short subway ride, hop on a boat, and be on a beautiful island (a Greek island!) within an hour? My favorite getaway is beautiful little Hydra—walk up narrow streets lined with stone mansions, hike across herb-scented countryside to a monastery, take a dip in the rocks, and be back in Athens in time for dinner. *See p 89.*

⑬ Browsing the Central Market. Big, noisy, smelly, and fragrant, this market's indoor and outdoor stalls bring together all the food of Greece, from exotic denizens of the deep to country cheeses and swinging carcasses. For me, just looking at all these riches is one of the city's culinary experiences, even if I don't

Produce on sale at Central Market.

leave the premises with anything more adventurous than a plastic bag of olives (the most delicious in the world). *See p 81.*

⑭ Gazing out to sea from the Temple of Poseidon. You only have to make the pleasant trip down the Attic coast to Sounion to appreciate how ancient Greeks gave rise to the concept that location is everything. It's easy to see how the sight of the majestic temple warmed the hearts of sailors returning to Athens after months at sea. *See p 20.*

⑮ Coming upon Kapnikarea Church. This little Byzantine gem sits right in the middle of Ermou Street, and just setting eyes on the old stones and carvings immediately transports you away from the contemporary buzz to a different time and place. *See p 20.* ●

The Odeon of Herodes Atticus.

1 The Best **Full-Day Tours**

8

The Best **in One Day**

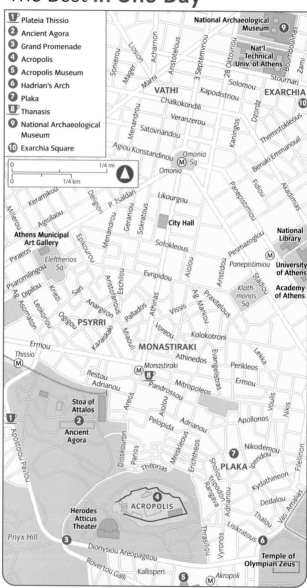

1. Plateia Thissio
2. Ancient Agora
3. Grand Promenade
4. Acropolis
5. Acropolis Museum
6. Hadrian's Arch
7. Plaka
8. Thanasis
9. National Archaeological Museum
10. Exarchia Square

Previous page: A statue of a discus thrower in Athens.

Even if you've set your sights on a sunny Aegean island, you will not want to overlook the city that gave rise to much of western culture. Give yourself at least a day to explore this sprawling metropolis, where all you have to do is lift your eyes to gaze upon the symbol of the Golden Age of Greece, the Acropolis. A day hardly does justice to the city, but it will be enough time to see many of the masterworks of the ancient world, and to get a sense of modern Greek life as well. START: **Thissio Square. Metro: Thissio.**

1 ★★ **Plateia Thissio.** Begin the day as many Athenians do, lingering over a coffee and a "toast" (a grilled cheese or grilled ham-and-cheese sandwich) at a cafe. Athinaion Politeia (33 Apostolou Pavlou and 1 Akamantos sts.; ☎ 210/341-3795) and other cafes on this animated square afford views of the Ancient Agora, the Acropolis, and across the city, Lycabettus Hill. ⏱ *30 min. Apostolou Pavlou and Iraklidon sts. $.*

2 ★★ **Ancient Agora.** The center of commercial, administrative, and social life in ancient Athens is today a jumble of broken columns and crumbling foundations strewn among olive, pink oleander, cypress, and palm trees. The sole remaining ancient structure is the Hephaisteion, the best-preserved Greek temple in the world, from the 5th century B.C. The Stoa of Attalos is a mid-20th-century reconstruction, but all the same evokes the

days when St. Paul preached Christianity here and Socrates sat on a bench expounding his philosophical principles. ⏱ *1 hr. See p 34.*

3 ★★★ **Grand Promenade.** A cobblestone-and-marble, pedestrian-only boulevard skirts the Acropolis Hill, providing a stroll through the millennia all the way from the Agora (p 34) to Hadrian's Arch (p 31). Follow the walkway through scented pine, olive, and cypress groves around the base of Filopappou Hill, then make the ascent for a close-up look at the Acropolis through the Beule Gate. ⏱ *15 min. See p 26.*

4 ★★★ **Acropolis.** The beloved, 2,400-year-old landmark of Greece's Golden Age stands high above the city (Acropolis means "High City"), an enduring symbol of perfection that instills pride in even the most hard-nosed Athenians and awe in their visitors. Wars, plunder, pollution, and neglect have taken their toll on the

For 2,400 years, a climb to the Acropolis has proven to be a peak experience for visitors.

The entrance to the Acropolis Museum overlooks the Makriyanni excavation site.

Parthenon, the harmonious temple to Athena, and the smaller monuments that surround it on the hilltop. Even so, in its sun-bleached beauty, the Acropolis continues to show the heights to which a civilized society can aspire. ⏱ *2 hr. See p 22.*

5 ★★★ **Acropolis Museum.** The sculptures and statuary that once adorned the temples of the Acropolis—a breathtaking presence through the tall windows—are shown to beautiful advantage among acres of glass and marble. Caryatids (sculptures of women taking the place of columns or architectural supports), statues of *korai* (maidens) dedicated to Athena, figures of *kouri* (young men), and elaborate friezes—4,000 works altogether—are displayed in the light-filled

The Plaka is brimming with souvenirs and shoppers.

galleries. What's not here are many segments of the Parthenon Frieze, carted off to England from 1801 to 1804. Greece wants these treasures back, and stunning quarters on the museum's top floor await their return. ⏱ *2 hr. See p 28.*

6 ★★ **Hadrian's Arch.** This beautifully preserved, albeit soot-darkened, triumphal arch was erected in honor of the emperor in A.D. 131. The monument then divided the old Greek city from the new Roman city that Hadrian, an ardent Hellenophile, endowed with many temples and monuments. Hadrian considered Athens to be the cultural capital of the Roman Empire and struck his claims to the city by having the marble on the east side of the arch inscribed with "this is the city of Hadrian and not of Theseus" and the west side with "This is Athens, once the city of Theseus." ⏱ *10 min. See p 31.*

7 ★★ **Plaka.** The sprawling old quarter beneath the Acropolis is a remnant of 19th-century Athens, with Byzantine churches and the occasional fragment of the ancient city sprinkled among the narrow lanes. With alleys, simple, bougain-villea-clad houses, and a round-the-clock holiday atmosphere, the Plaka also exudes the cheerful ambiance of a Greek island. Vendors hawk souvenirs (especially along Adrianou and Pandrossou streets), chicly clad young Athenians sit in cafes alongside their worry-bead wielding elders, and waiters try to lure passersby into restaurants serving some of the city's most undistinguished cuisine. It's easy to feel you've stumbled into a tourist trap as you amble through the Plaka, but this colorful heart of old Athens is quintessentially and alluringly Greek. ⏲ *1 hr. See p 60.*

8 Thanasis. It's best to stick to simple fare when eating in the Plaka. Thanasis or any of the other psistaries ("cookhouses") on Mitropoleos Street dispense delicious kebabs (juicy slices of souvlaki with yogurt sauce served in a pita) for about 2€. *$.*

You will probably want to take the Metro (to Victoria Station) or trolley to the museum, but the walk through Omonia (p 66) introduces you to the bustle of downtown Athens. The best route takes you north from the Plaka to Omonia on Aiolou, an animated pedestrian walkway.

9 ★★★ National Archaeological Museum. The splendor of ancient Greece comes to the fore in the world's finest collection of Greek antiquities. Galleries behind the neoclassical facade are filled with sensuous marble statues that once adorned temples throughout Greece and other treasures that span Greek history from the age of Homer to the days of the Roman empire. Three collections steal the spotlight: the gold death mask and other treasures that Heinrich Schliemann excavated in the royal tombs at Mycenae in 1876; the colorful Minoan frescoes buried during a volcanic eruption on the island of Santorini around 1600 B.C.; and the sinuous marble figures that Cycladic peoples fashioned 5,000 years ago. In winter, the museum closes at 3pm Tuesday to Sunday, so adjust your timing accordingly. ⏲ *2 hr. See p 38.*

10 ★ Exarchia Square. You might want to head back to your hotel to collapse, but if you still have stamina, walk to Exarchia, the student quarter just south of the museum. The neighborhood's proximity to the Polytechnic university makes it a magnet for artists, intellectuals, and hordes of youth who frequent the cafe-bars and shops around the square. A student uprising in Exarchia on November 17, 1973, left 34 dead but eventually brought down Greece's oppressive military dictatorship. ⏲ *30 min. Stournari and Themistokleous sts.*

The National Archaeological Museum.

The Best **in Two Days**

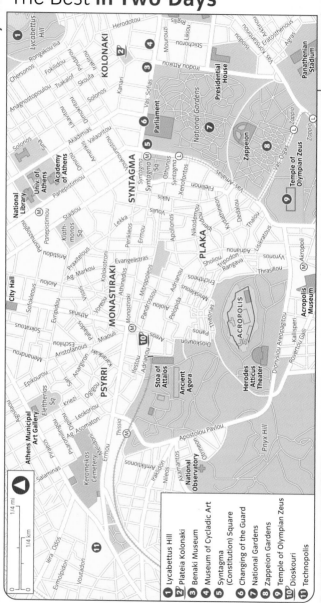

1 Lycabettus Hill
2 Plateia Kolonaki
3 Benaki Museum
4 Museum of Cycladic Art
5 Syntagma (Constitution) Square
6 Changing of the Guard
7 National Gardens
8 Zappeion Gardens
9 Temple of Olympian Zeus
10 Dioskouri
11 Technopolis

A second day in Athens gives you the pleasure of discovering more vistas, quiet corners, and a hefty array of fascinating history and art collections. You won't be straying too far afield, and just about all the stops on this itinerary are within walking distance of one another on and around Syntagma Square. START: **Teleferik (funicular) station in Kolanaki. From Syntagma walk west to Kolanaki on Vassillissis Sofia or take bus 22, 60, or 200 to the Teleferik.**

1 ★ kids **Lycabettus Hill.** One of the most popular rides in town is aboard the Teleferik that climbs to the pine-clad summit of the highest hill in Athens. Legend has it that Lycabettus is actually a piece of rock that Athena intended to use to make her temple on the Acropolis even loftier; she became distracted while winging her way over the city and dropped it, doing us all a favor. The views of the Acropolis and across endless blocks of white buildings to the sea are mesmerizing. ⏲ 1 hr. See p 65.

2 ★ **Plateia Kolonaki.** The Teleferik drops you back in Kolonaki, a shady enclave where you'll probably get the impression that the well-heeled residents do nothing but shop or sit at the cafes around Kolonaki Square. Take a seat at a cafe of your choice, and enjoy a frappe (a tasty concoction of Nescafe and frothy milk) while watching the endless parade of elegant, beautifully coiffed elderly women, well-fed businessmen, wafer-thin models, and nattily attired young men on the prowl. ⏲ 30 min. $. See p 64.

3 ★★ **Benaki Museum.** Antonis Benakis (1873–1954) used his enormous wealth to collect classical statues, Hellenistic jewelry, Byzantine icons, early Christian textiles, paintings by El Greco, mementoes of the War of Independence— that is, anything Greek. More than 20,000 pieces are displayed in the family mansion and a modern wing. ⏲ 1 hr. See p 64.

A ceramic pitcher from the Benaki Museum, one of about 40,000 items on display there.

The highest point in Athens, Lycabettus Hill rises above the Kolonaki quarter.

The changing of the guard takes place hourly in front of Parliament on Syntagma Square.

4 ★★★ **Museum of Cycladic Art.** One of Greece's early civilizations produced elegant, almost abstract marble figures that seem strikingly modern and were an inspiration to such 20th-century sculptors as Picasso, Modigliani, and Brancusi. Greece's wealthiest shipping dynasty, the Goulandris family amassed more than 300 of these figures, housed in light-filled modern galleries. The adjoining Stathatos Mansion, an opulent creation of 19th-century German architect Ernest Ziller, houses temporary exhibitions and warrants a walk through no matter what's on view. 🕐 *1 hr. See p 64.*

5 ★ **Syntagma (Constitution) Square.** The heart of Athens takes its name from the constitution that unpopular sovereign Otto of Bavaria was forced to adopt after an uprising in 1843. Otto's imposing palace at one end of the square is now the seat of Parliament. Make your way through the hordes of young Athenians who congregate around the splashing fountain, then descend into the metro station-cum-museum for a look at the many Greek, Roman, and Byzantine artifacts unearthed during excavations. A

mound of earth behind a glass wall is especially poignant—a skeleton, segments of a road, and other bits and pieces reveal century after century of human enterprise on the site. 🕐 *30 min. See p 57.*

6 ★★ **kids** **Changing of the Guard.** The two soldiers *(evzones)* who stand guard over the Tomb of the Unknown Soldier in front of Parliament ceremoniously change places with their replacements every hour or so. Guards are chosen for their height and looks and put on quite a show: Attired in short pleated skirts, red shoes with pompoms, and tasseled red caps—said to replicate the garb Greek revolutionaries wore during the 1820s War of Independence—they go through a choreographed routine of slow-motion high kicks that seems almost like a surreal dance. 🕐 *15 min. See p 53.*

7 ★ **National Gardens.** Queen Amalia, wife of King Otto, almost started another revolution back in the mid–19th century when she banned the Greek public from using the 16 hectares (40 acres) of paths, ponds, gardens full of exotic plants, and shady lawns behind her palace. The gardens have been open to all since 1923 and are a welcome refuge from the swirl of traffic just outside the gates. ⏲ *15 min. See p 53.*

8 ★ Zappeion Gardens. This shady oasis adjoining the National Gardens is crisscrossed by broad promenades and surrounds the Zappeion, a vast, neoclassical exhibition hall put up for the 1898 Olympics and intended to re-create the monumental buildings of ancient Athens. Step inside for a look at the spectacular oval atrium, enclosed by a two-story colonnade of columns and caryatids. ⏲ *15 min. See p 45.*

9 ★★ Temple of Olympian Zeus. The greatest monument that Roman emperor Hadrian bestowed upon his beloved Athens (p 32) is this massive temple, the largest in Greece, completed in A.D. 131. Hadrian finished the work that the tyrant Peisistratos began in the mid-500s B.C. but abandoned for lack of funds. ⏲ *30 min. See p 31.*

10 Dioskouroi. Take a well-deserved rest before setting out to explore Athens by night. Begin with a walk through the Plaka and a drink and some meze on the terrace of this pleasant cafe overlooking the Agora and the Acropolis. *37–39 Adrianou St. (look for the logo of an ancient ship logo on the awnings).* ☎ *210/325-3323 or 3333. Drinks and snacks about 15€. $$.*

11 ★★ Technopolis. Old brick smokestacks that once infamously spewed toxic fumes now glow with colored lights and provide a beacon above the increasingly hip Gazi neighborhood—Gazi translates as "gas lands," a reference to the unwelcome effect this former gasworks once had on the surroundings. The city of Athens converted the complex to an arts and culture center in the late 1990s (Technopolis means "Arts City"), and brick and stone-walled exhibition spaces surround a courtyard that is often used for concerts. One hall houses the Maria Callas Museum, allowing a voyeuristic peek at some of the diva's personal effects and clothing. The main exhibition spaces at Technopolis are usually open until 9pm; for a late dinner (early by Greek standards), move on to one of the many restaurants and cafes that have sprung up in Gazi and adjoining Psyrri. ⏲ *1 hr. See p 59.*

Soaring columns still pay homage to the supreme god at the Temple of Zeus.

The Best **in Three Days**

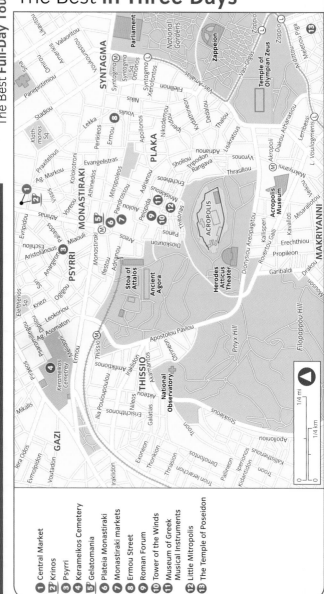

1 Central Market
2 Krinos
3 Psyrri
4 Kerameikos Cemetery
5 Gelatomania
6 Plateia Monastiraki
7 Monastiraki markets
8 Ermou Street
9 Roman Forum
10 Tower of the Winds
11 Museum of Greek Musical Instruments
12 Little Mitropolis
13 The Temple of Poseidon

Day three begins in a place close to the heart of all Athenians, the bustling Central Market. Stock up on some portable comestibles, then begin a walking tour that will reveal many sides and eras of this complex city, from the here and now to the ancient past. Old and new are piled on top of the other in Athens, so any walk like this one becomes a journey through time. START: **Central Market, Athinas Street near Omonia Square. Metro to Omonia.**

Athenians stock up on fresh fish and other staples at the Central Market.

1 ★★ **Central Market.** The sheep heads, live chickens, calf carcasses, and other wares probably won't tempt you, and even much of the snack food on offer, such as steaming bowls of tripe soup, can seem a bit, uh, exotic. But few places in Athens are livelier and more colorful, and the scent of wild herbs wafting through the vast halls is transporting. The heaping piles of comestibles provide a culinary tour of Greece: You probably never knew there were so many kinds of olives or varieties of creatures in the sea. Cheese, bread, sliced meats, and other picnic fare are sold at the north end of the market. The market opens at 6am Monday through Saturday and should be in full swing by the time you arrive in the morning. ⏲ *30 min. See p 81.*

2 **Krinos.** Athenians have been making this cramped cafe a mandatory morning stop since the 1920s.

Loukoumades (fritters sprinkled with cinnamon and drizzled with honey) are the specialty, though boughasta (cream pies) and other treats also emerge from the kitchen. *Aiolou 87, Central Market.* ☎ *210/321-6852. 2€. $.*

3 ★★ **Psyrri.** Many nocturnal habitués of Athens's trendiest neighborhood wouldn't recognize the narrow lanes and squares by the light of day. You'll have to come back after dark to see the bars and clubs in full swing, but on a daytime walk through this once run-down warren of workshops and little houses you can appreciate the picturesque charms of one of the city's last remaining 19th-century enclaves. The neighborhood's current reputation for debauchery is entirely in keeping with tradition—Psyrri was long known as a haven for underworld thugs and as a hotbed for revolutionaries. ⏲ *30 min. See p 63.*

Trendy Psyrri is bustling with street vendors peddling jewelry and other wares.

4 ★★★ **Kerameikos Cemetery.** From the 7th century B.C. to the 1st century A.D., Athenians of means and status were laid to rest in this extensive city of the dead, preferably on the remarkably well-preserved Street of Tombs. In antiquity, Kerameikos was a busy crossroads where all roads to Athens converged at the Dipylon Gate, the largest gateway in ancient Greece; traces of this monumental entryway remain, as do the city walls that Themistockles erected in 478 B.C. and once extended from Kerameikos as far as the port at Piraeus. The well-preserved Sacred Gate was reserved for pilgrims arriving for the Panathenaic Festival, who followed the Sacred Way from Kerameikos to the Agora and up to the Acropolis. 🕐 *1 hr. See p 34.*

5 **Gelatomania.** Though you've just indulged your sweet tooth at Krinos, you can't come to Psyrri without tasting the best gelato in Athens, made on the premises. *Aisopou 21.* ☎ *210/323-0001. 2€. $.*

You can follow Ermou Street about 10 blocks east to Plateia Monastiraki, or take the Metro; Monastiraki is just one stop away from Kerameikos station.

6 ★★ **Plateia Monastiraki.** This lively square, paved in gold mosaics, takes it name from a medieval monastery and poorhouse of which only the church of Panayia Pantanassa remains. More prominent is the tiled-domed 18th-century Tzistarakis Mosque, a remnant from the days of Ottoman rule, and infamously linked with a desecration—a Turkish administrator destroyed a column from the Temple of Olympian Zeus to extract lime for the

The Tzistarakis Tzami mosque on Monastiraki Square.

Busy Ermou is one of the city's main shopping streets.

construction, and a plague soon swept through the city. You can step beyond the porch into several halls that display beautiful Turkish ceramics. ⏱ *30 min. See p 58.*

7 ★★ **Monastiraki markets.** A Turkish bazaar grew up around the Tzistarakis Mosque, and narrow alleyways leading off the square, especially Ifestou and Pandrosou streets, still have a souklike feel to them and are lined with stalls and tiny shops. The exotic aura is especially in evidence on Sunday mornings, when a flea market snakes along Ifestou and nearby Kyntou and Adrianou streets. ⏱ *30 min. See p 81.*

8 ★ **Ermou Street.** Ermou is closed to traffic between Monastiraki and Syntagma and one of the cities most popular shopping venues, an endless parade of department stores, specialty shops, and antiques dealers. You will strike gold if you are in the market for footwear, since Ermou is especially popular with shoemakers (p 80). Should you become weary of commercialism, you can take refuge in Kapnikarea, a handsome little 10th-century

An Ancient Soap Opera

Watching the sea and the distant Peloponnesian mountains fade into the sunset ether from the Temple of Poseidon may well put you in the mood to ponder the myth of Theseus. The Athenian youth was sent to Crete to be sacrificed to the Minotaur in the maze of King Minos, but the king's daughter, Ariadne, fell in love with him and gave him a sword to slay the Minotaur and a ball of fleece he could unravel to find his way out of the maze. The pair set sail for Athens, but Theseus abandoned Ariadne on the island of Naxos. The jilted Ariadne put a curse on Theseus, and under her spell, he changed the sails of his ship to black (a sign he had died). His father, Aegeus, saw the black-sailed ship approaching from Sounion, assumed his son was dead, and leapt from the cliff into the sea that to this day bears his name.

The frieze atop the Tower of the Winds in the Roman Agora depicts Greek wind deities.

church that sits right in the middle of the street. ⏲ *30 min. See p 58.*

⑨ ★★ Roman Forum. When the Romans took Athens in the 1st century B.C., Julius Caesar and Augustus decreed that the Ancient Agora (p 34) was too crowded and relocated the center of commerce to an airy courtyard surrounded by an arcade of shops. Their names are inscribed on the Gate of Athena Archegetis, and the Ottomans left their mark with the beautiful, 15th-century Fethiye Mosque, built to celebrate their conquest of Athens. ⏲ *1 hr. See p 63.*

⑩ ★★★ Tower of the Winds. The most remarkable structure in the forum predates the Roman marketplace, built by Syrian astronomer Andronikos Kyristes around 50 B.C. The octagonal tower is the best-preserved Roman monument in Athens and one of the most distinctive buildings of the ancient world. Each of the eight sides

is inscribed with images of Boreas and other personifications of the winds; a water-propelled clock at the top of the tower, no longer there, was powered by a stream running down the Acropolis Hill and was one of the great scientific achievements of ancient Rome. ⏲ *15 min. See p 33.*

⑪ ★ Museum of Greek Popular Musical Instruments. The lyres and other instruments on display here are beautifully crafted, and headphones deliver a pleasant introduction to centuries of Greek music. Better yet, the museum occasionally hosts concerts of traditional music in its attractive courtyard. ⏲ *30 min. See p 41.*

⑫ ★★ Little Mitropolis. The Mitropolis, cathedral of Athens, is justifiably important as the center of the Greek Orthodox Church, but its tiny, 12th-century neighbor, Panagia Gorgoepikos (unofficially Little Mitropolis) steals the show. Reliefs of animals and zodiac signs cover the exterior walls, and a miraculous painting of the Virgin Mary resides inside. ⏲ *15 min. See p 61.*

⑬ ★★★ kids The Temple of Poseidon. In mid- to late-afternoon, set out by bus (either by public service or on an organized tour) for Cape Sounion, a promontory at the southern tip of the Attica Peninsula. Here, in 444 B.C., the statesman Pericles (who also built the Parthenon) commissioned the Temple of Poseidon atop a seaside cliff. Little remains except 15 Doric columns, fashioned from marble quarried nearby in the Agrileza Valley. For ancient sailors, a sighting of the temple meant they were nearing home; for today's visitors, climbing to the ruins to enjoy the view over a broad sweep of the Aegean can be one of the most memorable experiences of their travels in Greece. The outlook from the temple is famously spectacular (and popular) at sunset. ⏲ *4 hr. See p 91.* ●

The **Acropolis**

1 Beule Gate
2 Propylaia
3 Temple of Athena Nike
4 Erechteion
5 The Parthenon

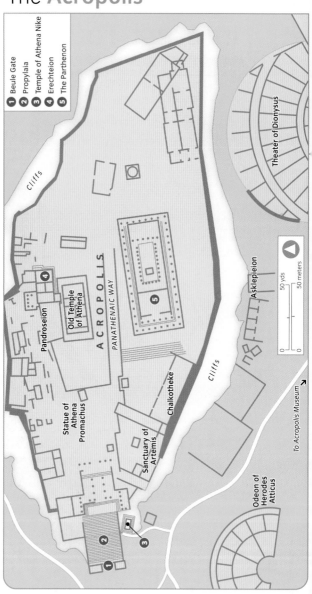

Cliffs

Theater of Dionysus

ACROPOLIS

PANATHENAIC WAY

Pandroseion

Old Temple of Athena

Statue of Athena Promachus

Asklepieion

Cliffs

Chalkotheke

Sanctuary of Artemis

Odeon of Herodes Atticus

To Acropolis Museum

0 50 yds
0 50 meters

Previous page: The mosaic of the Madonna and Child at the door of the circa 11th-century Kapnikarea church on Ermou Street.

The great emblems of classical Greece, and arguably the most important ancient monuments in the Western World, have loomed above Athens for 2,500 years. Cast your eyes from just about anywhere in the city below and you are likely to catch a glimpse of the marble temples that the statesman Pericles erected atop the Acropolis hill in the 5th century B.C.; the sight of these monuments gleaming in the sun never fails to inspire awe and renew our faith in civilization and the ideals that fostered such perfection. Even better is climbing to the top of the hill for a close-up look, one of the most rewarding experiences you'll have in Greece, or anywhere. Allow at least 2 hours to explore the Acropolis. START: **Beule Gate, off Grand Promenade. Metro to Acropolis.**

Acropolis Tips

The Acropolis is located at Dionysiou Areopagitou Street. Admission is 12€, is valid for 5 days, and also includes admission to the Ancient Agora, Theater of Dionysos, Kerameikos Cemetery, Roman Forum, Hadrian's Library, and the Temple of Olympian Zeus. There is an elevator for visitors with disabilities. The Acropolis is open to visitors from April to October daily 8am to 7:30pm, and November to March daily 8am to 3pm. Call ☎ 210/321-0219 or visit www.culture.gr for more information.

❶ ★ **Beule Gate.** From the ticket pavilion just off the Grand Promenade, a path ascends to this grandiose entryway built by the Romans in A.D. 280 and named for the French archaeologist who unearthed the monumental entryway in 1852. Don't be misled by the inscription on the lintel from 320 B.C.—the gate incorporates fragments from an earlier monument. In the days of Pericles, the Acropolis was entered on the Sacred Way, a processional walkway that crossed the city from Kerameikos and ascended the Acropolis via a series of ramps and steps. Just beyond the gate is a

A temple to Athena, crowning the Acropolis Hill above Athens, has long exemplified classical perfection.

The Vision of Pericles

The Acropolis was inhabited at least 5,000 years ago, and for early Athenians the flat-topped, 156m-high (520-ft.) outcropping provided protection and views of enemies approaching by sea and across the surrounding plains. Such measures proved powerless against the Persians, who razed Athens, and the Acropolis with it, in 479 B.C. Athenians and Spartans banded together to rout the Persians in 449 B.C., and a year later the great general and statesman Pericles set about rebuilding the Acropolis. He hired the sculptor Pheidas and the architects Iktinos and Kallikrates, plundered the state coffers, and with the aid of the finest artisans of the day, the purest marble, and a workforce of thousands, completed the Parthenon within 10 years and most of the other temples and monuments within a decade or two later.

The perfectly proportioned Parthenon and its neighbors on the Acropolis were showpieces for the superiority of Athens and the achievements of a Golden Age that fostered democratic ideals, the philosophy of Socrates, the plays of Aeschylus and Sophocles, and the artistry of Praxitelis and other sculptors. Pericles bankrupted Athens by building the Acropolis, and by 404 B.C. the city had fallen to the Spartans. But the harmony and proportion Pericles achieved on the Acropolis Hill has survived the ages.

pedestal that during the Roman years was topped with a secession of statuary honoring charioteers, Anthony and Cleopatra, and finally, Marcus Agrippa, the general who defeated the couple's forces at the Battle of Actium.

2 ★★ **Propylaia.** Ancient visitors to the Acropolis passed through this symbolic entryway, an antechamber to the sacred precincts beyond. A central hall housed five gates; one was reserved for priests, worshippers, charioteers, and beasts who made their way up the Acropolis in a long procession during the Panathenaic Festival (depicted in the Parthenon Frieze, p 28). A forest of elegant columns remains in place, including a double row that surrounds the inner porch and dramatically frames the Parthenon, just beyond. A portion of the paneled ceiling and fragments of frescoes hint at the Propylaia's former grandeur and the awe it must have inspired in those passing through these halls.

3 ★★ **Temple of Athena Nike.** This miniscule shrine is tucked next to the Propylaia on a vertigo-inducing platform at the edge of the Acropolis Hill. Square and perfectly proportioned, with four columns at either end, the temple honors Athena in her guise as the goddess of victory and was built between 427 and 424 B.C. as a prayer for success against Sparta in the Peloponnesian War.

4 ★★★ **Erechtheion.** Perhaps the most distinctive of all Greece's ancient temples stands on the spot where Poseidon and Athena allegedly squared off in a contest to see who would be honored as patron of the city. Poseidon struck his trident into a rock and unleashed a spring, while Athena topped him by miraculously producing an olive tree, symbol of lasting peace and prosperity (much valued but short-lived in 5th-century-B.C. Athens). Marks of Poseidon's trident can be seen in a rock on the north porch, and an olive tree still grows nearby. The god and goddess are honored in the temple, built on three levels to accommodate the slope of the Acropolis Hill and supported in part by caryatids, maidens delicately draped in pleated gowns that take the place of columns; the ones in place are copies and five of the originals are in the Acropolis Museum (p 28).

Four Caryatids ("maiden" columns) supporting a porch on the Erechtheion.

5 ★★★ The Parthenon. The sacred sanctuary to Athena and storehouse of the treasury of the Delian League stands at the highest point of the Acropolis. Two of the temple's most remarkable features are no longer here—an 11m-tall (36-ft.), gold-plated statue of the goddess by the great sculptor Pheidas, and the 160m (530-ft.) Parthenon Frieze; segments are in the Acropolis Museum (p 28) and others, carted off to London by Lord Elgin between 1801 and 1805, are in the British Museum (see p 28 for more on the ongoing battle to bring these treasures back to Greece). Much the worse for wear—battered by looting, the elements, pollution, and an explosion and fire ignited by Venetian artillery in 1687—the majestic temple is still the symbol of artistic perfection. With a sharp eye you might detect a trick of optical illusion; since straight lines appear curved, Parthenon architects slightly curved and bowed the temple's 50 columns so they seem to be perfectly straight.

The Acropolis Walkway skirts the bottom of the Acropolis Hill and connects many of the city's ancient sights.

Along the **Grand Promenade**

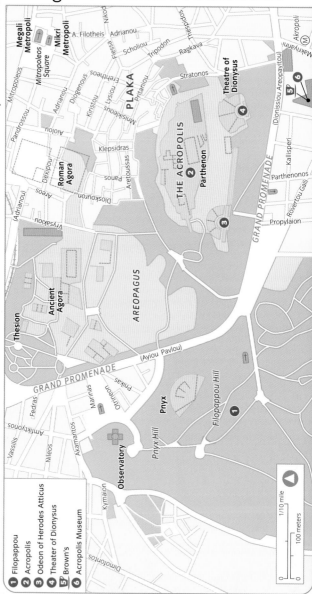

1. Filopappou
2. Acropolis
3. Odeon of Herodes Atticus
4. Theater of Dionysus
5. Brown's
6. Acropolis Museum

1/10 mile

100 meters

A walkway of marble and cobblestone skirts the base of the Acropolis Hill, linking some of the world's most famous ancient sites and providing Athenians and their visitors a pleasant stroll through pine-scented parkland. You can follow the walkway all the way from Hadrian's Arch (p 31) to Plateia Thissio (p 9); this walk takes in a cluster of landmarks in close proximity to the Acropolis. START: **Thissio Square. Metro: Thissio.**

1 ★★ **Filopappou.** This hilly precinct just west of the Acropolis affords stunning, eye-level views of the Parthenon. In fact, the view has been mesmerizing gazers since the days of Pericles, when the general assembly (Ecckesia) met on the Hill of the Pnyx; any citizen of Athens could vote on civil matters, making this a hallowed ground of early democracy. An even better outlook is from the summit of the adjacent Lofos Mousson (Hill of the Muses). Follow Dimitriou Aiginitou off the Grand Promenade. ⏲ *1 hr. See p 86.*

2 ★★★ **Acropolis.** In ancient times, worshippers and celebrants made the ascent to the Acropolis on a series of grand ramps and staircases. The current approach, along a well worn path through the Beule Gate, is no less inspiring, given the fabled ruins that lay ahead. ⏲ *1 hr. See "The Acropolis" tour, p 22.*

3 ★ **Odeon of Herodes Atticus.** Wealthy statesman, scholar, and philanthropist Herodes Atticus funded works throughout Greece, including the baths at Thermopylae and a theater in Corinth. In A.D. 160 he presented this lovely theater to the Athenians in memory of his wife, Regilla. Since a 1955 restoration, audiences fill the 34 rows of seats for drama, music, and dance performances of the Athens and Epidaurus Festival (p 128). You may visit the theater only during performances, but you will see portions of the arched exterior and get a sense of the theater's elegant proportions on a walk around the pine-scented grounds.

⏲ *30 min. Grand Promenade, Thrassilou and Dionysiou Areopagitou sts.*

4 ★★ **Theater of Dionysus.** A theater has been tucked into the slope of the Acropolis Hill since the 6th century B.C., when Athenians began celebrating a Dionysus Festival to honor the god of wine and ecstasy with several days of dancing, feasting, and drinking. Celebrations became more refined during the 5th-century B.C. Golden Age, and theatergoers came from throughout to see the dramas of Aeschylus, Sophocles, and Euripides. The ruins you see today are of a vast marble theater begun in 342 B.C. that sat 17,000 spectators on 64 tiers of marble benches; 20 rows remain, as does a claw-footed throne, carved with satyrs, that was reserved for the priest of Dionysus. ⏲ *45 min. Grand Promenade, Thrassilou and Dionysiou Areopagitou sts.* ☎ *210/322-4625.*

Biking along the Grand Promenade.

The Frieze Fracas

Fifty panels of the Parthenon Frieze, the remarkably animated marble frieze of maidens, priests, soldiers, worshippers, and oxen making their way to the Acropolis to honor the goddess Athena, are in the British Museum in London. Lord Elgin, onetime British ambassador to the Ottoman Empire, began removing segments of the frieze in 1801, supposedly with the permission of Turkish officials, and shipped them home. Greece is demanding the return of the treasures, carrying on a campaign that actress and minister of culture Melina Mecouri launched in the 1980s. Britain's long-standing argument that Greece can't properly care for the treasures wanes with completion of the stunning new galleries awaiting their return.

www.culture.gr. Admission 2€ or part of Acropolis ticket. Apr–Oct daily 8am–7:30pm, Nov–Mar 8am–3pm.

⑤ **Brown's.** Before you tackle the formidable collections of the Acropolis Museum, enjoy a snack or meal at this cafe and restaurant with eye-popping views of the Parthenon from the terrace and glass-enclosed dining room. *Acropolis Museum.* ☎ *210/900-0915. $$.*

⑥ ★★★ **Acropolis Museum.** Glass walkways, acres of marble, and airy views of the Parthenon provide a stunning

backdrop for the friezes and sculptures from the 5th-century B.C., Golden Age heydays of the Acropolis Hill. Also on view are pediment pieces from temples, statues, and fragments of temples that adorned the Acropolis before Pericles went on his Acropolis building spree, as are statues of Alexander the Great and other works commissioned for the Acropolis in the centuries after Pericles through the Roman occupation. The treasures (4,000 pieces in all) and the stunning contemporary quarters that house them do justice to the great achievements of ancient Greece. *See mini-tour on following page.*

The Odeon of Herodes Atticus.

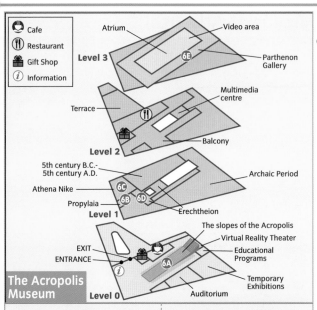

The Acropolis Museum

- Cafe
- Restaurant
- Gift Shop
- Information

Level 3 — Atrium, Video area, 6E, Parthenon Gallery

Level 2 — Terrace, Multimedia centre, Balcony

Level 1 — 5th century B.C.–5th century A.D., Athena Nike, Propylaia, 6C, 6B, 6D, Erechtheion, Archaic Period

Level 0 — EXIT, ENTRANCE, 6A, The slopes of the Acropolis, Virtual Reality Theater, Educational Programs, Temporary Exhibitions, Auditorium

A walk through the Acropolis Museum's glass and stone galleries mimics an ascent up the Acropolis Hill. On the ground floor, the **6A Acropolis Slopes** gallery houses votives, offerings, and other finds from sanctuaries at the base of the Acropolis where cults to Athena and other gods and goddesses worshipped; an overlook provides a look at ruins in situ beneath the museum. The marble floor gently slopes toward the next level, where works are arranged in the order in which ancients walking through the Acropolis would have encountered them: a head of Hermes, by Alkamenes, in the **6B Propylaia collections** once greeted visitors passing through the ceremonial entrance way; in the **6C Temple of Athena Nike exhibit,** a relief captures the goddess in the refreshingly humanlike act of unfastening her sandal; and in the **6D Erechtheion** section, five famous Caryatids, female figures used in place of columns on the temple's south porch, are grouped on a balcony. In the top floor **6E Parthenon Galleries,** friezes and metopes are arranged as they appeared on the temple, in full view through the floor-to-ceiling windows. One of the world's greatest ancient treasures wraps around the walls: the Frieze of the Great Panathenaia (also known as the Parthenon Frieze), a 160m-long (530-ft.) tableaux of a procession in honor of Athena. ⏱ *2 hr. 15 Dionysiou Areopagitou St.* ☎ *210/900-0900. www.the acropolismuseum.gr. Admission 5€, 3€ students and children under 18. Tues–Thurs and Sat–Sun 8am–8pm, Fri 8am–10pm.*

Ancient Athens

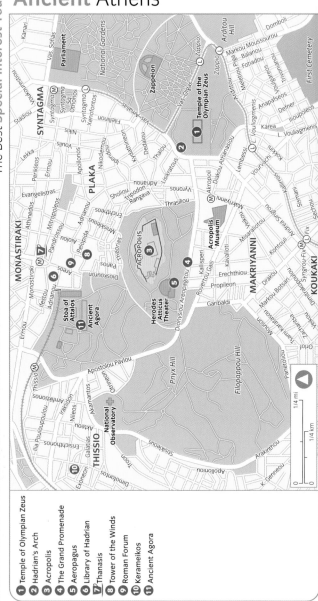

1 Temple of Olympian Zeus
2 Hadrian's Arch
3 Acropolis
4 The Grand Promenade
5 Aeropagus
6 Library of Hadrian
7 Thanasis
8 Tower of the Winds
9 Roman Forum
10 Kerameikos
11 Ancient Agora

The ruins of the Agora, the Roman Forum, and the other monuments that cluster around the base of the Acropolis attest to commerce, politics, learning, and the other foundations of life in the seat of modern democracy. Among these thyme-scented stones it's easy to imagine hustle and bustle and even the elevated discourses of Socrates. You can take this journey back in time simply by following the Grand Promenade and stepping in and out of the many ancient sites along the route. START: **Metro to Acropolis.**

1 ★★ Temple of Olympian Zeus. Just beyond his monumental gateway, Hadrian completed the largest temple in the Greek world, commissioning his architects to pick up where the tyrant Peisistratos had left off in the 6th century B.C. The unfinished temple, with its vast foundations and huge columns, had lain abandoned for centuries and became a symbol of wanton extravagance; Aristotle held the temple up as an example of the excesses with which tyrants enslaved the populace. Hadrian may have been inspired to complete the temple after seeing two columns that the general Sulla took back to Rome in 81 B.C. and installed in the Temple of Jupiter on the Capitoline Hill. Hadrian's temple lacks the grace of the Parthenon but is undeniably impressive: 104 Corinthian columns, more than 1.5m (5 ft.) in diameter, stood 16m (52 ft.) tall; 15 remain in place and are dramatically floodlit at night. Hadrian installed a replica of the statue of Zeus by Phidias (sculpted for a temple to the god in Olympia and one of the Seven Wonders of the Ancient World) in the cella and immodestly erected a similarly sized statue of himself next to it. ⏱ *45 min. Vas. Olgas St. & Amalias Ave.* ☎ *210/922-6330. www.culture.gr. Part of the 12€ Acropolis ticket package or admission 2€. Apr–Oct daily 8am–7:30pm, Nov–Mar daily 8am–5pm. Metro: Syntagma or Akropoli.*

2 ★ Hadrian's Arch. The 2nd-century Roman Emperor, an ardent Philhellene, expanded the city east of the Themistoclian Walls and named the district he created after himself, Hadrianoupolis. This grand entryway, dedicated in A.D. 131, was the demarcation between old and new Athens—as an inscription on either side of the graceful central arch proclaims. The gate is remarkably well preserved, though ignobly besieged by a swirl of passing traffic. ⏱ *10 min. Amalias Ave. and Dionysiou Areopagitou St.*

3 ★★★ kids Acropolis. A climb to the top of the city's sacred mount is one of the world's most rewarding travel experiences (see "The Acropolis" tour, p 22).

4 ★★★ kids The Grand Promenade. A walk around the foot of the Acropolis Hill on this beautiful

The Temple of Zeus.

Hadrian's Arch (see p 31).

avenue brings you to the Theater of Dionysus, the Odeon of Herodes Atticus, and the Acropolis Museum (see "Along the Grand Promenade" tour, p 26).

⑤ ★ kids Areopagus. A bald granite outcropping next to the Acropolis, reached by treacherous steps carved out of the rock, is one of the most ancient and storied places in Athens. According to legend, the gods tried Ares here for killing Halirrhothios, son of Poseidon. Ares was acquitted on the grounds that he was protecting his daughter from the unwanted advances of Halirrhothios. The summit was the meeting place of the Council of the Areopagus, an assembly of citizens who heard murder trials, and for

Socrates and his students, who were able to discourse away from the distractions of the city. St. Paul delivered his famous Sermon to an Unknown God from atop the Areopagus, trying to convert Athenians to Christianity. You may well encounter pilgrims from around the world who climb the hill to pay homage to Paul. ⏱ *20 min. Continuation of Theorias St. opposite Acropolis entrance. Metro: Akropoli or bus: 230.*

⑥ ★ Library of Hadrian. Roman emperor Hadrian built this lavish hall, of which a portion of a columned porch remains, for learning, discourse, and relaxation. At the center of the complex was a large inner court, surrounded by

City of Enlightenment

For almost 1,500 years—from around 900 B.C. to A.D. 500— Athens was one of the most important cities in the ancient world, a center of trade and for many centuries renowned for promoting art and philosophy. Much of the ancient city you see today was built or transformed by the Romans, who gave Athens free status and financed many public works. Athens enjoyed the favor of Hadrian and other Roman emperors until the 6th century, when Justinian, a Christian, declared the famous schools of philosophy to be pagan institutions and closed them.

100 columns supporting a portico overlooking the courtyard's garden and pool. Lecture halls, rooms for reading and conversation, and a library where papyri were stored in stone cabinets (a few of which survive) opened off the court. Hadrian intended the library to be his contribution to the intellectual life of Athens; he and other Romans considered the city to be the Empire's center of learning and enlightenment, and many noble families sent their sons to Athens to be educated. 🕑 *15 min. Closed to public; can be viewed from Aiolou St.*

From the Areopagus, it's easy to find a rocky perch from which to contemplate the past while taking in the sprawl of modern Athens.

7 Thanasis. Just follow the crowds to the most popular souvlaki restaurant in the Plaka and enjoy a delicious and inexpensive lunch at one of the outdoor tables. *Metropolis 69.* ☎ *210/324-4705. $.*

8 ★ kids Tower of the Winds. One of the most intriguing buildings of the ancient world stands on high ground next to the Roman Forum. With a weather vane and eight sundials visible from afar, the structure was one of the first known versions of a clock tower. Friezes of the eight winds decorate each side, and inside was a water clock that employed gears and sophisticated mechanisms to regulate the flow of water from a stream on the Acropolis Hill into a basin, allowing timekeepers to make measurements. 🕑 *30 min. See p 20.*

9 ★ Roman Forum. The well-preserved Gate of Athena Archetegis is inscribed with a notice that these now-ruined monuments—a

The Agora, the commercial hub of the ancient city, became so congested that an annex, the Roman Forum, was built nearby.

rectangular marketplace that was the commercial center of the city under the many years of Roman rule—were erected with funds from Caesar and Augustus. Hadrian, who rebuilt so much of Athens in the 2nd century, is represented in the forum by a simple inscription regulating the sale of oil at the bazaar that operated near the entrance. In the 16th century, when Athens fell to the Ottomans, Mehmed II the Conqueror was allegedly so taken with the classical beauty of the city that he prohibited destruction of the ancient monuments on pain of death. He converted the Pantheon to a mosque and built the Fethyie (Victory) mosque on the north side of the forum to celebrate his conquest. ⏱ *30 min. Aiolou & Pelopida sts.* ☎ *210/324-5220 or 210/321-0185. Part of the 12€ Acropolis ticket package or admission 2€. Daily May–Oct 8am–7pm; Nov–Apr 8:30am–3pm. Metro: Monastiraki.*

⑩ ★ Kerameikos. Potters settled Kerameikos (from which the word ceramics is derived) as early as 1200 B.C. and by the 7th century B.C. the district had become the main burying ground of Athens. Generations of noble Athenians were laid to rest along the Street of Tombs, beneath monuments that seem little affected

A detail from the Ancient Agora.

by the millennia—including a splendid marble bull atop the tomb of Dionysos of Kollytos and a marble relief of Dexileos, showing the young soldier on horseback preparing to spear an opponent (ironically mimicking his own death at the hands of the Corinthians in 394 B.C.). Not as well preserved are two gates in the ruins of the city walls that Themistocles erected in 478 B.C.: The Dipylion Gate was the main entrance to the city, while the Sacred Gate was reserved for participants in sacred processions. Pottery, funerary sculptures, and other finds from Kerameikos are displayed in the Oberlaender Museum, next to the entrance. ⏱ *1 hr. 148 Ermou St.* ☎ *210/346-3552. Admission part of the 12€ Acropolis ticket package. Museum & site 2€. Mon–Sun 8am–7:30pm. Metro: Thissio.*

⑪ ★ Ancient Agora. For almost 1,000 years, starting in the 6th century B.C., much of Athens's day-to-day life transpired in this commercial, administrative, and social quarter. The senate met here, philosophers argued (the stoas—porticos—of the Agora lent their name to stoicism), and the city elite gathered to watch the ceremonial processions that passed through the Agora on the Sacred Way. In fact, so important was the Agora in the life of ancient Greece that it was ground zero, the point from which all distances throughout the Greek world were measured. ⏱ *1 hr. Entrance/exit on Adrianou St. & Agiou Filippou, Monastiraki; west end of Polygnotou St., Plaka; & Thissio Sq., Thissio.* ☎ *210/321-0185. www.culture.gr. Site & museum part of the 12€ Acropolis ticket package or admission 4€. May–Oct daily 8am–7pm, Nov–Apr daily 8am–4pm. Metro: Monastiraki or Thissio.* See mini-tour on following page.

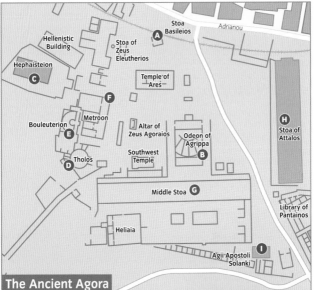

The Ancient Agora

With a little imagination, a perusal of this ruin-strewn site will reward you with a sense of life at the center of Ancient Athens. The **A** **Stoa Basileios** housed the offices that administered the many ancient cults that worshipped specific gods and goddesses. A serpent-tailed giant and two Tritons stand next to what was the entrance to the **B** **Odeon of Agrippa,** a small theater built by the Roman official of the same name in A.D. 15. The beautifully preserved **C** **Temple of Hephaestus** was devoted to Athena and Hephaestus, god of blacksmiths, and surrounded by metalworking shops; a beautiful frieze atop the 34 columns depicts Hercules and Theseus, ancient Greece's popular superheroes who slew beasts and monsters and performed other amazing feats. The government's ruling body met and lived in the circular **D** **Tholos,** while the council met in the nearby **E** **Bouleuterion** and state archives were kept in the **F** **Metroon.** Athens's temple to Zeus was built outside the Agora in the 4th century B.C. but moved to a prominent place in front of the **G** **Middle Stoa,** with columned porticoes sheltering dozens of market stalls. The **H** **Stoa of Attalos** was the city's major shopping venue, with marble-paved colonnades that were popular gathering places; the two-story stoa was reconstructed in the 1950s and houses pottery, oil flasks, bronze disks used to cast votes, and many other finds evoking commercial and political life in the ancient city. Just behind is a beautiful medieval landmark, the 11th-century **I** **Agii Apostoli Solanki (church of the Apostles).** See p 49.

Top Museums in Athens

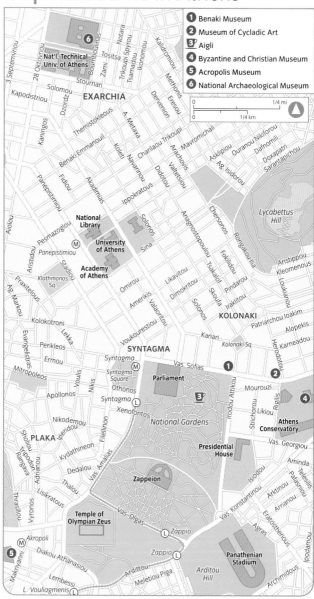

1 Benaki Museum
2 Museum of Cycladic Art
3 Aigli
4 Byzantine and Christian Museum
5 Acropolis Museum
6 National Archaeological Museum

The many ages of Greek culture come to the fore in the museums of Athens, some of the finest collections of their kind in the world. You won't want to come to the capital without visiting these five standouts, where you'll witness Greek civilization from the dawn of recorded history through the end of the Byzantine Empire. START: **Metro to Monastiraki.**

① ★★ Benaki Museum. Antonis Benakis (1873–1954) spent his vast fortune satisfying his taste for anything having to do with Greek heritage, spanning the millennia from prehistory to the 20th century. More than 20,000 objects are showcased in the Benaki family's 19th-century mansion and a modern wing. Mycenaean and Roman jewelry, 5,000-year-old gold and silver bowls that mark the transition from the Stone Age to the Bronze Age, pistols Lord Byron brandished when he came to Greece in 1824 to join the fight for independence, and paintings by El Greco (who left his native Crete for Spain) are among the treasures you'll come across in the 36 rooms. Especially intriguing are reception rooms, plush with paneling and Persian carpets, from an Ottoman mansion in Macedonia that have been painstakingly re-assembled. A rooftop cafe overlooking the National Gardens (p 53) is a great place to recharge, and the gift shop is stocked with beautiful reproductions of silver, terra-cotta, and jewelry. 🕐 *1 hr. Koumbari 1.* ☎ *210/367-1000. www.benaki.gr. Admission 6€ adults, 3€ seniors and students. Mon, Wed, Fri, Sat 9am–5pm, Sun 9am–3pm, Thurs 9am–midnight. Metro: Evangelismos.*

② ★★ Museum of Cycladic Art. A walk through these attractive modern galleries provides a wonderful encounter with the enigmatic marble figurines left behind by a culture that flourished in the Cycladic islands from 3200 to 2000 B.C. More than 350 figures are elegantly simple and symmetrical—elements not lost on such modern masters as Picasso and Modigliani, who were hugely inspired by these pieces. Most are female, suggesting they were sculpted in honor of a goddess, though a few warriors and other males slip into the mix. Additional exhibits bring together vases, lamps, tools, and other artifacts for an

Art on display at the Benaki Museum.

enlightening and entertaining look at everyday life in classical Greece, and temporary exhibitions are mounted in an adjoining 19th-century neoclassical mansion by Ernst Ziller, who designed many municipal buildings in Athens and elsewhere in Greece (p 64).

🕐 *1 hr. 4 Neophytou Douka St.* ☎ *210/722-8321 or 210/722-8323. www.cycladic.gr. Admission 7€ adults, 3.50€ seniors and students. Mon, Wed, Fri–Sat 10am–5pm; Thurs 10am–8pm; Sun 11am–5pm. Metro: Syntagma or Evangelismos.*

3 **Aigli.** Take a breather from museum going with a walk through the National Gardens (p 53) with a stop for a drink and a snack on the shady terrace of this popular cafe. *National Garden.* ☎ *210/336-9300. $$.*

4 **Byzantine and Christian Museum.** From their palaces in Constantinople, Byzantine emperors and the hierarchy of the Orthodox church ruled much of the Balkans and Asia Minor from the 6th century well into the 15th century. Few collections anywhere match the trove of icons, manuscripts, frescoes, mosaics, and sculptures the period

Poseidon from the National Archaeological Museum.

The Cup Bearer sculpture at the Museum of Cycladic Art.

produced. One of the most enchanting pieces is an ivory depicting a lyre-playing Orpheus surrounded by animals, an allegorical reference to Christ and his followers that was typical of the transition from paganism to Christianity. Mosaic floors from a 5th-century basilica and a Roman villa show similar refinement and sophistication, a testament to how Byzantine masters kept classical artistry alive through the Dark Ages.

🕐 *1 hr. 22 Vasilissis Sofias Ave.* ☎ *210/721-1027. www.byzantine museum.gr. Admission 4€. Apr–Sept Tues–Sun 8am–7:30pm; Oct–Mar Tues–Sun 8:30am–3pm. Metro: Evangelismos.*

5 ★★★ **Acropolis Museum.** The full impact of the Golden Age comes to light in these stunning glass-walled galleries that showcase sumptuous friezes and statuary from the Parthenon and other temples. *See p 28.*

6 ★★★ **National Archaeological Museum.** The achievements of Ancient Greece are revealed in gallery after gallery of one of the world's great museums. Sensuous statues of athletes and maidens, rare bronzes, frescoes, and brightly painted vases all bring the ancient Greek world to life—an exhilarating yet overwhelming experience you may well wish to spread out over a couple of visits.

🕐 *3 hr. 44 Patission & 28 Oktovriou sts.* ☎ *210/821-7717. www.na museum.gr. Admission 7€ adults, 18 & under free. Mid-Apr–mid-Oct Mon 1–7:30pm; Tues–Sun & holidays 8am–7:30pm. Mid-Oct to mid-Apr Mon 1–7:30pm; Thurs 8:30am–7:30pm; Tues–Wed, Fri–Sun & holidays 8:30am–3pm. Metro: Victoria or trolley: 2, 3, 4, 5, 6, 7, 8, 9, 11, 13, 15.*

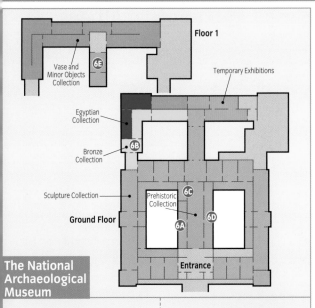

The National Archaeological Museum

Some of the most moving images from the ancient world are captured in the National Archaeological Museum's **6A funerary monuments,** including one from the Grave of Aristonautes in Kerameikos (p 59), in which a boy tries to refrain a frisky horse. While most of ancient Greece's bronze statues were melted down for weaponry over the centuries, three extraordinary **6B bronzes** were retrieved from shipwrecks: Marathon Boy depicts a youth, perhaps a young Hermes; a majestic figure from around 400 B.C. may be Poseidon or Zeus—his hands are clasped to hold a missing piece that may have been a thunderbolt or a trident; and a galloping steed with a horseman astride its back. The **6C Mycenaean Collection** evokes the short-lived civilization that dominated much of the southern Mediterranean from around 1500 to 1100 B.C. and whose king, Agamemnon, launched the Trojan War and inspired the

legends of Homer. The Myceneans left behind gold death masks and many other magnificent treasures, unearthed by Heinrich Schliemann in the 1870s. While the Museum of Cycladic Art (p 64) shows off more of the enigmatic marble figures typical of this early civilization, on display in the **6D Cycladic Collection** here are some three-dimensional pieces, including an utterly charming harp player, and a life-size female figure that is the largest Cycladic piece yet to be unearthed. The **6E Thira Collection** showcases frescoes from the Minoan settlement of Akrotiri on Santorini (also known as Thira), buried in a volcanic eruption around 1600 B.C.; images of monkeys (indicating trade with North Africa), ships sailing past leaping dolphins, cows, and young women gathering saffron reveal much about everyday life in such a distant past and are hauntingly beautiful.

Small Museums in Athens

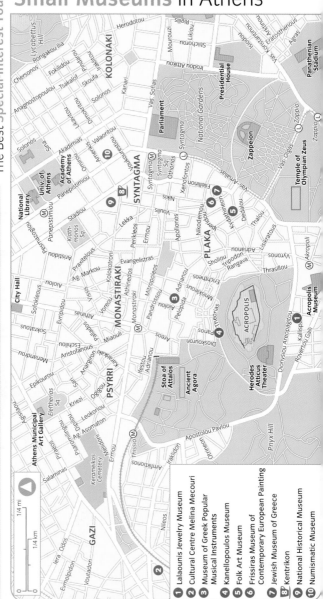

1 Lalaounis Jewelry Museum
2 Cultural Centre Melina Mecouri
3 Museum of Greek Popular Musical Instruments
4 Kanellopoulos Museum
5 Folk Art Museum
6 Frissiras Museum of Contemporary European Painting
7 Jewish Museum of Greece
8 Kentrikon
9 National Historical Museum
10 Numismatic Museum

While the National Archaeological Museum and Acropolis Museum get much deserved attention, don't overlook some of the city's other great but less-heralded treasures. Athens is richly endowed with dozens of smaller museums that preserve Greek culture in all its many facets, from jewelry to music. The collections are remarkable, and exploring them provides an informative, entertaining, and often surprising look at Greek life.

START: **Metro to Monastirak.**

❶ ★ Lalaounis Jewelry Museum.

Greece's millennia-long knack for crafting fine jewelry comes to the fore in the workmanship and style of internationally renowned designer Ilias Lalaounis (b.1920). His magnificent gold and silver interpretations of Greek designs, inspired by cultures from the Minoans to the Ottomans, are displayed in the former Lalaounis workshops, alongside jewels and bling from around the world. The designer's dazzling pieces are on offer in the museum shop, but don't look for prices any lower than they are at the other tony Lalaounis shops around the world. ⏱ *30–45 min. 4 Karyatidon & 12 Kallisperi sts.* ☎ *210/922-1044. www.lalaounis-jewelrymuseum.gr. Admission 5€. Mon & Thurs–Sat 9am–4pm; Wed 9am–9pm; Sun 11am–4pm. Metro: Akropoli or bus: 230.*

❷ Cultural Centre Melina Mecouri.

Take a romp through 19th-century Athens along a typical street of the then-newly transformed capital, painstakingly re-created in a former hat factory. Shop windows display clothing and dry goods, a door opens into a neoclassical house, and a *kafeneion* (coffeehouse) is so authentic you can almost hear the clatter of worry beads. The center evokes the memory of Melina Mecouri (1920–94), the actress and former minister of culture who launched the battle for the return of the Parthenon Marbles (p 28). ⏱ *30 min. Iraklidon 66a.* ☎ *210/345-2150. Free admission.*

Tues–Sat 9am–1pm and 5–9pm, Sun 9am–1pm. Metro: Petralona.

❸ ★ kids Museum of Greek Popular Musical Instruments.

With roots in the ancient world and the Byzantine and Ottoman Empires, Greek music goes far beyond the *Never on Sunday* theme that wandering minstrels pluck out in tourist tavernas. Gorgeously crafted instruments, recorded music, and occasional live performances deliver a delightful introduction to Greek musicology. ⏱ *30 min. 1–3 Diogenis St.* ☎ *210/325-0198. Admission free. Tues, Thurs–Sun 10am–2pm; Wed noon–6pm. Metro: Monastiraki.*

A display at the Museum of Greek Popular Musical Instruments.

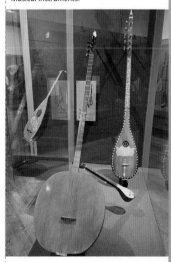

4 Kanellopoulos Museum. Enjoy a pleasant, low-key introduction to the panorama of Greek art, from prehistory to 19th-century independence, in a fine 19th-century mansion in Anafiotika. Cycladic sculptures, terracotta cult figurines, a 2nd-century-B.C. marble head of Alexander the Great, icons, and other pieces amassed by 20th-century Athenians Pavlos and Alexandra Kanellopoulos are shown off in lovely salons beneath paneled ceilings. ⏱ *30 min. 12 Theorias St. at Panos St.* ☎ *210/321-2313. Admission 2€. Tues–Sun 8:30am–3pm. Metro: Monastiraki.*

A bust of Alexander the Great in the Kanellopoulos Museum.

puppets used in traveling shows, and festive costumes show some wonderfully fanciful flourishes, too. Frescoes by Theophilos Hatzimihail, a naïve artist who lived and worked on the island of Lesbos, cover the walls of one room, and the collection spills over into the Tsisdarakis Mosque and the Loutro ton Aeridon (Bathhouse of the Winds), one of the last of the Turkish *hamams* that the Ottomans installed throughout Athens. ⏱ *30–45 min. 17 Kydathineon St.* ☎ *210/322-9031. Admission 2€. Tues–Sun 9am–2pm. Metro: Syntagma.*

5 Folk Art Museum. These baskets, homespun textiles, pottery, and hand-hewn tools elevate even the simplest everyday items into works of art—and suggest just how labor-intensive rural life once was. But pillows that brides-to-be embroidered for the marital bed, jewelry,

An exhibit at the Folk Art Museum.

6 Frissiras Museum of Contemporary European Painting. Should you begin to think that Greek art ended some time around 400 B.C., step into these stark galleries spread across two adjoining neoclassical mansions for a look at the work of contemporary Greek artists, as well as those from other European countries. Some of the works by David Hockney and other internationally known artists will be familiar, but you will also enjoy an introduction to Costas Tsoclis and other highly acclaimed Greek artists. ⏱ *30–45 min. 3 and 7 Monis Asteriou St.* ☎ *210/323-4678. www. frissirasmuseum.com. Admission 6€, 3€ seniors and students. Wed–Fri 10am–5pm; Sat–Sun 11am–5pm. Metro: Syntagma.*

7 Jewish Museum of Greece. Jews have lived in Greece since ancient times, and by the 18th century Jewish communities thrived throughout the mainland and islands; Thessalonika, in fact, was one of the world's great centers of Jewish

Frissiras Museum of Contemporary European Painting.

culture. Manuscripts, textiles, and everyday household objects cover the span of Jewish life in Greece, which was all but obliterated during World War II—the period is hauntingly evoked with personal effects of many of those deported to death camps. ⏲ *30–45 min. 39 Nikis St.* ☎ *210/322-5582. www.jewish museum.gr. Admission 5€, students 3€. Mon–Fri 9am–2:30pm; Sun 10am–2pm. Metro: Syntagma.*

⑧ Kentrikon. A cozy cafe under the shopping arcades across from the National Historical Museum serves grilled meats, stews, and other traditional favorites to a crowd of lunchtime regulars. *3 Kolokotroni St.* ☎ *210/323-2482. $.*

⑨ National Historical Museum. *Palaia Vouli,* or Old Parliament (housing the Greek Parliament from 1875–1935), is the suitable home for collections that focus largely on the Greek War of Independence, idealistically captured with such mementoes as the sword and helmet Lord Byron donned when he came to Greece to take up the cause. Less than idealistic realities of the nation's past are also depicted in galleries surrounding the former assembly chamber, from the harsh yoke of Ottoman rule to the Battle of Crete. ⏲ *30–45 min. 13 Stadiou St. at Kolokotroni St.* ☎ *210/323-7617. www.nhmuseum. gr. Admission 3€. Tues–Sun 9am–2pm. Metro: Syntagma.*

⑩ Numismatic Museum. A chance to step into the former home of Heinrich Schliemann, the archaeologist who unearthed Mycenae and Troy, is much of the appeal, but don't let the spectacular surroundings detract from the extraordinary coins on display—600,000 in all, dating from 700 B.C. Many of the coins are arranged by the themes depicted on them, so you can loiter over the cases to compare the charming representations of gods and goddess, Roman generals and Byzantine emperors, and mythical beasts and sea creatures. ⏲ *30 min. 12 Panepistimiou St.* ☎ *210/364-3774. www. nma.gr. Admission 3€. Tues–Sun 8:30am–3pm. Metro: Syntagma.*

The neoclassical Iliou Melathron mansion is home to the Numismatic Museum.

Architectural Athens

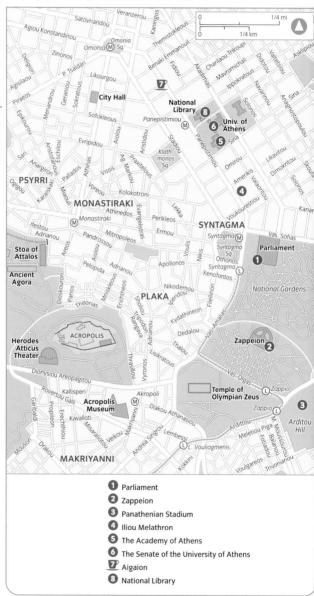

1 Parliament
2 Zappeion
3 Panathenian Stadium
4 Iliou Melathron
5 The Academy of Athens
6 The Senate of the University of Athens
7 Aigaion
8 National Library

You may get the impression that Athenian architecture comes in just two varieties, ancient ruin and modern sprawl, but look again. The ever-growing city has managed to protect a wealth of 19th-century neoclassical landmarks, erected when the modern, independent Greek state was just taking shape. START: **Metro to Syntagma.**

❶ Parliament. The palace that Munich architect Friedrich von Gaertner built for King Otto in 1848 probably did not do much to endear the unpopular monarch to his Greek subjects. Almost fortresslike, the massive, austere landmark is a formidable presence on Syntagma Square, perhaps befitting its present role as home to the Greek Parliament. Two highly photogenic soldiers in traditional *foustanellas* (ceremonial skirtlike garments) who guard the Tomb of the Unknown Soldier are among the few signs of life. ⏱ *15 min.*

❷ Zappeion. Amid the nationalistic fervor of the newly formed Greek nation, millionaire Evangelias Zappas sought to build a hall to host worldfair-style exhibitions as well as ceremonies for a revival of the Olympic Games. Theophilos Hansen, who had demonstrated his neoclassical bent in his designs for the Greek Academy (p 46) and National Library (p 47) designed the huge, semicircular hall, inaugurated in 1888 and named for

the man who had financed the project. Hansen adorned the long facade with a portico and an elegant row of columns, but his pièce de résistance lies within—a vast circular atrium surrounded by a two-story arcade supported by columns and Caryatids. The Zappeion was the venue for fencing competitions during the first revival of the Olympic Games in 1896, and in more recent years has been the scene of ceremonies signing Greece into the European Union. ⏱ *20 min. Entrances from the National Gardens, Amalias Ave. & Vas. Olgas & Vas. Konstantinou sts. Daily 9am–5pm (hours vary depending on events). Free admission. Metro: Syntagma.*

❸ Panathenian Stadium. A stadium built around 330 B.C. to host the Panathenian games has been well used over the millennia. Greco-Roman aristocrat Herodes Atticus had the stadium reconstructed in A.D. 143–144, and the so-called Kalimarmaro (Beautiful Marble) underwent another redo by architect Ernst Ziller

The striking Parliament building, on Syntagma Square.

A City Transformed

After Greece's War of Independence, Otto of Bavaria, then just 17, was named sovereign. One of his first orders of business was to transform what was then just a small town into a grand European capital. He imported some of the most prominent northern European architects of the day to design palaces and public buildings in a neoclassical style in honor of the ancient culture whose enduring landmarks loom above the city on the Acropolis as inspiration. While Otto's Athens never attained the grandeur of Baron Haussmann's Paris, the city is all the better for his efforts. We can only hope that the opening of the Grand Promenade (p 26) early in this century is a sign of more urban transformation to come.

and Anastasios Metaxa to host the first modern Olympic Games in 1896. The stadium is still used for events, and during the 2004 Olympics hosted the archery competitions and was the finish line for the marathon. For a look at a 21st-century sporting venue, head to Irini Metro station to see the 2004 **Olympic Stadium,** 37 Kifissias Ave. (☎ 210/683-4060; www.oaka.com.gr), with a beautiful sweeping roof by Spanish architect Santiago Calatrava. ⏲ *10 min. Vas. Konstantinou & Irodou Attikou sts. Metro: Acropolis.*

❹ **Iliou Melathron.** Heinrich Schliemann, the German archaeologist who unearthed the ancient kingdoms of Troy and Mycenae, commissioned German architect

The Zappeion exhibition hall in the Zappeion Gardens is symmetrically arranged around a circular interior atrium.

Ernst Ziller to design his Athens residence, which he named Iliou Melathron (Palace of Troy). Ziller emblazoned the gates with swastikas (a popular design in ancient Greece) and decorated the cavernous interior with marble, columns, and ancient-looking frescoes—just the right setting in which the learned Schliemann could entertain his dinner guests by reciting the *Iliad* from memory. The splendid rooms are enhanced by the presence of the holdings of the Numismatic Museum, one of the world's finest collections of ancient and historic coins (including many from Troy and Mycenae). ⏲ *30 min. See p 64.*

❺ **The Academy of Athens.** In the 1840s, Danish architects Theopolis and Christian Hansen came to Athens to take up Bavarian King Otto's mandate to rebuild the new capital in neoclassical style. They focused their energies on three adjoining buildings that are now surrounded by more functional buildings of the University of Athens. Theopolis undertook the Academy, where two 23m-tall (75 ft.) tall columns topped with statues of Athena and Apollo flank the entrance portico, which is much embellished with statuary—most elaborate is the

The National Library, third in a trilogy of neoclassical buildings by the Hansen brothers.

pediment frieze depicting the birth of Athena. In the main hall, beneath frescoes of the myth of Prometheus, is a statue of Simon Sinas, Greek consul to Vienna and philanthropist who bankrolled the project; it's only fitting that Hansen took his inspiration from the Parliament in Vienna, which he also designed, adding a few flourishes from the Erechtheion on the Acropolis (p 24). The Academy, still in residence, promotes the advancement of sciences, humanities, and fine arts, and the public may step in for a look at the main hall and library. ⏱ *10 min. 28 Panepistimiou St. ☎ 210/360-0207, 210/360-0209, or 210/364-2918. Free admission. Mon–Fri 9am–2pm. Metro: Panepistimiou.*

6 The Senate of the University of Athens. Christian Hansen, the brother of Theophilos, was King Otto's court architect and in 1839 began work on what was to be the main building of the National and Kapodistrian University, now referred to simply as the University of Athens. Hansen was well versed in a classical sensibility, and also spent his time in Athens reconstructing the Temple of Nike on the Acropolis (p 24). He showed more restraint with the Senate than his brother did with the two buildings flanking it, adorning the refined facade with a graceful, tall portico. ⏱ *10 min. 30 Panepistimiou St. ☎ 210/360-0209. www.uoa.gr. Free admission. Mon–Fri 9am–2pm. Metro: Panepistimiou.*

7 Aigaion. One of the city's favorite stops for sweet tooths makes *loukoumades* (deep fried fritters drizzled with honey and cinnamon) as well as the best rizogaio (rice pudding) in all of Greece. *26 Panepistimiou St. ☎ 210/381-4621. $.*

8 National Library. The third in the Hansen brothers' trilogy was designed by Theophilos, who indulged his bent for extravagance with a sweeping pair of curving marble staircases. It's well worth the effort to ascend them to see the exhibits in which the library shows some of Greece's most rare manuscripts, including fragments of 6th-century gospels and the earliest known versions of Homeric epics. ⏱ *10 min. 32 Panepistimiou St. ☎ 210/338-2601. www.nlg.gr. Free admission. Mon–Thurs 9am–8pm; Fri–Sat 9am–2pm. Metro: Panepistimiou.*

Byzantine Athens

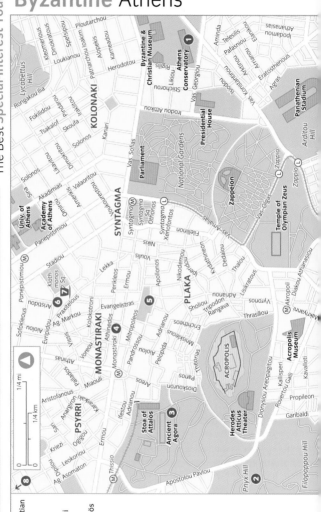

1. Byzantine and Christian Museum
2. Agios Dimitrios Loumbardiaris
3. Agii Apostoli Solanki
4. Kapnikarea
5. Panagia Gorgoepikoös
6. Agii Theodori
7. Alpeis
8. Daphni Monastery

Athens was an outpost of the Byzantine Empire for almost a thousand years, and the city's medieval churches are repositories of mosaics, frescoes, and icons created by Byzantine craftsmen. See their masterpieces in the outstanding Byzantine and Christian Museum, then in the city's relatively few remaining medieval churches that continue to hold their own against the onslaught of modern Athens. To see some of the finest Byzantine mosaics in the world, you need only make the short trip to the outlying Daphni Monastery. START: **Metro to Evangelismos.**

① Byzantine and Christian Museum. A visit to one of the world's top collections of Byzantine art will set the stage for the monuments you will see when you set out to discover this long-lived empire's influence on Greece. 🕐 1 hr. See p 38.

② ★★ Agios Dimitrios Loumbardiaris. Legend surrounds this lovely little 14th-century church nestled in a copse on Pnyx Hill. In 1645, so the story goes, the Ottoman commander of the Acropolis garrison planned to fire upon Christians gathering for services in honor of Saint Dimitrios. The night before the attack, lightning hit the cannon and gunpowder magazine and ignited an explosion that killed the commander but spared his Christian daughter. The humble stone and wood church is decorated with some delightfully primitive frescoes. 🕐 45 min. Apostolou Pavlou St., on the path opposite (south) the entrance to the Acropolis. Hours vary. Free admission. Metro: Akropoli or bus: 230.

③ Agii Apostoli Solanki. One of Athens's oldest churches was built in the Agora around A.D.1020 to honor St. Paul, who preached Christianity in the surrounding stoas and atop the nearby Areopagus Hill. The Ottomans and overly zealous 19th-century renovators all but obliterated the charm of the church, which was tenderly restored to its original form in the 1950s. A few fine early Byzantine frescoes remain in place, though some wall paintings are from the 17th-century, and moved here from a now-demolished church. 🕐 10 min. Dionysiou Areopagitou St., in the Ancient Agora. Hours vary. Free admission. Metro: Monastiraki.

Agii Apostoli Solanki church, with the National Observatory and Agia Marina in the background.

The Kapnikarea chapel is dedicated to the Virgin Mary, and a portrait of the Madonna and Child sits over the front entrance.

4 ★ Kapnikarea. One of the greatest pleasures of strolling through the crowded Plaka and Monastiraki is coming upon this 11th-century gem, planted right in the middle of busy Ermou Street. The stone, tile-domed church was

Panagia Gorgoepikoös is built largely of marble and contains various Greek, Roman, Byzantine, and early Christian reliefs, paintings, and icons.

built on the site of an ancient temple to Athena, incorporates Roman columns from the Forum, and escaped demolition twice as Athens began to burgeon in the middle of the 19th century—so, standing proud, slightly sunken beneath the level of the modern street, the landmark is an endearing testament to the city's long past. ⏲ *10 min. Ermou & Kapnikarea sts. Hours vary. Free admission. Metro: Monastiraki.*

5 ★ Panagia Gorgoepikoös. Though overshadowed by the unremarkable 19th-century Mitropoli (Metropolitan Cathedral) next door, this little church dedicated to the Virgin Mary Gorgoepikoös ("she who hears quickly") is much closer to the hearts of Athenians. The late 12th-century builders chose the site of an ancient temple to Eileithyia (goddess of childbirth and midwifery) and made use of the old stones and cornices. As you peruse the more than 90 stone reliefs, you'll be treated to layers of the past—some are ancient, depicting the Panathenaic games, others are Roman, and many are early Byzantine designs of plants and animals, brought here from other shrines around the city. ⏲ *10 min. Mitropoleos & Agias Filotheis sts. at Mitropoleos Sq. Hours vary. Free admission. Metro: Monastiraki.*

6 Agii Theodori. Marble tablets over the door date this squat church to the middle of the 11th century. With its sturdy stone walls and eight-sided, tile-roofed dome, the church has withstood bombardment during the War of Independence and other ravages and stands as a sentinel from another age above the bustle of the busy streets below. Many of the frescoes inside date from the 19th century, and some charming terra-cotta reliefs of plants and animals remain. ⏲ *10 min. Evripidou & Aristidou sts. at*

Klafthmonos Sq. Hours vary. Free admission. Metro: Panepistimiou.

7 Alpeis. At a table on the terrace of this small cafe, tasty souvlaki and other inexpensive fare comes with a view across a pleasant square to Agii Theodori. *7 Palaion Patron Germanou St. at Klafthmonos Sq.* ☎ *210/331-0384. $.*

8 Daphni Monastery. One of Greece's finest Byzantine monuments was founded in the 6th century on the site of a temple to Apollo and takes its name from the laurels associated with the god—he was smitten with the goddess Daphne, who became exhausted by his advances and was transformed into a laurel tree; you can still see one of the temple columns in a wall. A prime position on the busy route to Corinth has left the monastery vulnerable to sackings by medieval crusaders and some rough handling during the War of Independence. Yet the spectacular 11th-century mosaics remain intact, colorfully depicting saints, prophets, angels, and, from the center of the tall dome, Christos Pantokrator (Christ

The 11th-century Agii Theodori chapel has a domed, tiled Byzantine roof, common to many Christian churches in Athens.

in Majesty). Daphni is located west of Athens and can be an ordeal to get to. Allow plenty of time and check that it is open before setting out; restoration following an earthquake in 1999 continues. ⏰ *2 hr. Lera Odos, Attica.* ☎ *210/581-1558. www.culture.gr. Tues–Sun 8:30am–3:30pm (call or check website for hours). Bus: A16, B16, E16, E63, 801, 836, 845, 865, 866.*

The Byzantines in Athens

From the 4th to the 15th centuries, Greece was administered from Byzantium (later Constantinople, now Istanbul) as an outpost of the Byzantine Empire. Over those many centuries, craftsmen developed a distinct style that came to the fore in the monasteries and churches of the increasingly powerful Greek Orthodox Church. While Athens faded into the ether as a small village under the Byzantines, the relatively humble stone churches that the medieval faithful erected, often using the marbles and columns of ancient ruins as building materials, kept the flames of civilization burning. The Byzantine Empire came to an end in 1453, when Constantinople fell to the Ottomans.

Athens **with Kids**

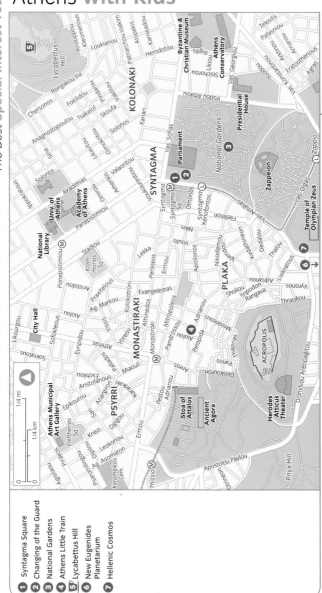

1 Syntagma Square
2 Changing of the Guard
3 National Gardens
4 Athens Little Train
5 Lycabettus Hill
6 New Eugenides Planetarium
7 Hellenic Cosmos

Children are practically worshiped in Greece, and you can take them to tavernas, restaurants, bars, and just about anywhere else you go—they'll probably enjoy most of what they see and do in Athens. The buzz of the pedestrian streets of the Plaka and Monastiraki can be pretty entertaining even to young travelers, and the ruins—especially those dramatically perched atop the Acropolis—will probably be as fascinating for them as they are for you. Here, too, are some sights and activities that will also probably be a hit with your young companions. START: **Metro to Syntagma.**

① ★★ **Syntagma Square.** The busy heart of Athens is surprisingly fun terrain for youngsters, with acres of traffic-free paving stones, refreshing fountains and pools, and some spiffy classical ruins unearthed during subway construction—including 1,800-year-old Roman baths covered by a glass roof. ⏱ *45 min. Amalias Ave. & Vas. Georgiou St. Daily 5:30am–midnight. Metro: Syntagma.*

② ★ **Changing of the Guard.** In front of Parliament at Syntagma Square, two *evzones* (traditionally dressed soldiers of the Presidential Guard) keep watch at the Tomb of the Unknown Soldier. Every hour on the hour, the guards do some pretty fancy footwork in front of the tomb. A much more elaborate duty-rotation ceremony occurs on Sunday at 11am. ⏱ *15 min. Amalias Ave. & Vas. Georgiou St. Metro: Syntagma.*

③ ★★ **National Gardens.** When the ruins get to be too much, escape into this welcome oasis of greenery behind Parliament. Duck and turtle ponds and a small zoo add a bit of excitement for kids not content just to sit on a bench. If you're not quite ready to hit the streets, explore the adjacent **Zappeion Gardens** (p 45), too. ⏱ *30 min. See p 14.*

④ ★★ **Athens Little Train.** Do some easy sightseeing aboard the *trenaki* (little train), which follows a circuit around the foot of the Acropolis and through the Plaka, Monastiraki, and other historic city-center neighborhoods. You and your young companions can hop on and off as often as you wish, taking in the sights until the whining starts. ⏱ *60 min. Terminal: Syntagma and Monastiraki Squares.* ☎ *210/725-5400. www.athenshappytrain.com.*

Syntagma Square supplies no end of amusements for young travelers.

Soldiers in foustanella and other military uniforms salute at the Tomb of the Unknown Soldier in Syntagma Square.

Adults 6€, children 9 & under 4€. Trains run every 30 min. 9am–midnight. Metro: Syntagma or Monastiraki.

5 ★ **Lycabettus Hill.** The views across the city to the Acropolis are mesmerizing, the pine-scented air is refreshing, and the ride up the 295m (965-ft.) outcropping aboard the Teleferik (cable car) is a good part of the fun. After a fortifying ice cream at one of the hilltop snack bars or carts, follow a path back down. *Teleferik: Aristippou & Ploutarchou sts.*

☎ 210/721-0701. Daily every 30 min. 9am–3am. Adults 6€ round-trip, 3€ one-way, children 7 & under 3€ (no credit cards). Bus: 022, 060 & 200.

6 ★ **New Eugenides Planetarium.** One of the world's most advanced star shows takes viewers to the moon (or, on another adventure, beneath the sea to explore a coral reef), with stunning 40-minute productions projected onto an enormous dome screen. ⏱ 1 hr. Eugenides Institute, 387 Syngrou. ☎ 210/946-9600. www.eugenfound.edu.gr. Wed–Sun 10am–8:30pm. Adults 8€, children & students 5€. Bus: 126, B2, A2 (from Akadimias St.), 550.

7 ★★★ **Hellenic Cosmos.** Learning ancient history doesn't get any more fun than it is at this high-tech media complex, where viewers take interactive, multimedia journeys through the Ancient Agora, encountering merchants, public officials, and soldiers along the way. ⏱ 2 hr. 254 Pireos St., Tavros. ☎ 212/254-5000. www.fhw.gr/cosmos. Admission 10€ adults, 8€ students and children. Oct–May Mon–Thurs 9am–2pm, Fri 9am–8pm, Sat 11am–4pm, Sun 10am–4pm; June–Aug Mon–Fri 9am–4pm, Sun 10am–3pm. Metro: Kalithea or Bus 194 (from Omonia; Athens School of Fine Arts stop). ●

"Little trains" ply a route through the city center, making it easy for kids and their adult companions to take in the sights.

Syntagma to Gazi

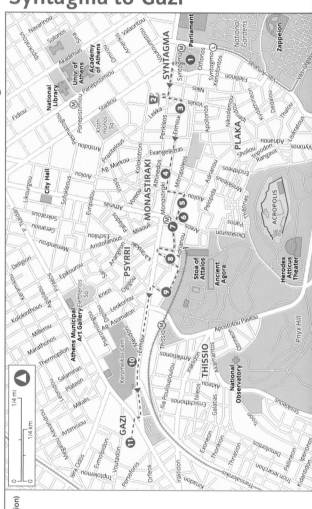

Previous page: An old doorway typical of the island-village-like neighborhood of Plaka.

You'll be in plenty of company on this walk, as it follows the main shopping thoroughfare along Ermou from Syntagma along the northern edge of the Plaka into busy Monastiraki and trendy Gazi. The Acropolis and other ancient ruins come into view as you move through these neighborhoods, but what you'll most enjoy is getting a look at day-to-day life in the appealing center of the modern city. START: **Metro to Syntagma.**

Syntagma Square.

❶ ★★ **Syntagma (Constitution) Square.** This lively expanse of paving stones, overlooked by the formidable Parliament building, is figuratively and literally the center of Athens. Parliament was once the palace of Otto of Bavaria, the first monarch of a newly independent Greece, and under his less-than-stellar leadership the first constitution was adapted in 1843. Ever since, the square has been a hallowed ground of Greek nationalism, a stage for protests, celebrations, and as you'll no doubt observe, the comings and goings of everyday life in the capital. Syntagma is also geographically at the center of Athens. Tree-lined Vasillis Sofias, the city's Museum Row—home to the Museum of Cycladic Art (p 64), the Benaki Museum (p 64), and several other collections—leads off the Square to the east. Plaka and Anafliotika, two of the city's oldest neighborhoods,

are just to the south; Omonia, the commercial center, is to the north; and the old working class neighborhoods of Monastiraki and Gazi are to the west. Before you hurry off to explore, though, stop to take a peek at the ruins of Roman baths unearthed during construction of the Metro; more artifacts are on display inside the modernistic station—a wonderful introduction to the juxtaposition of the ancient and the modern that you'll often encounter in Athens. 🕐 *20 min. Amalias & Vas. Georgiou sts. Metro: Syntagma.*

❷ **Ariston.** One of the oldest pita bakeries makes vegetable-and-meat-pies, deliciously stuffed with such combinations as chicken, leek, and eggplant, for about 2€. Take-out only. *10 Voulis St.* ☎ *210/322-7626. $.*

❸ ★★★ **Ermou Street.** One of the grand avenues of 19th-century Athens has blessedly been relieved of car traffic, making leisurely strolling and window shopping much more enjoyable than it once was. Department stores, big name international retailers, and expensive boutiques have a monopoly on the prime Ermou real estate, but small shopkeepers hold their own on the little lanes leading off in all directions. ⏱ *15 min. See p 80.*

❹ ★ **Kapnikarea.** One of the most charming sights in all of Athens is this little stone church from 1050—all the more remarkable since it sits smack dab in the middle of Ermou Street. Ludwig of Bavaria, father of Greece's King Otto, intervened to save the church from demolition in 1834, and the Bishop of Athens again halted destruction in 1863, ensuring the landmark a place on the Athenian landscape. The name refers to a Byzantine era tax but the church is dedicated to the Virgin Mary, just as the temple upon whose foundations it was built honored Athena or Demeter, two

Kapnikarea church.

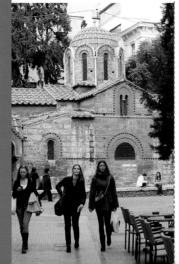

beneficent goddesses of ancient Greece. ⏱ *10 min. See p 50.*

❺ ★ **Pandrossou Street.** A short jog off Ermou Street onto **Aiolou Street** (named for Aeolus, god of wind) presents you with a nice view of the Roman-era Tower of the Winds, one of the world's first clock towers (p 33). Turn off Aiolou into Pandrossou, a pedestrian alley that was the Turkish bazaar and is one of the city's few vestiges of the 400 years of Ottoman rule that ended in the 1820s. A bazaarlike aura still prevails, and the narrow lane is chockablock with little souvenir and jewelry shops. ⏱ *10 min. Pandrossou St. at Mitropoleos Sq.*

❻ ★★ **Tzisdarakis Tzami.** Another remnant of the Ottoman presence is this handsome 18th-century mosque, now an outpost of the Museum of Greek Folk Art that shows off magnificent ceramics. Figurines, tiles, and bowls and other everyday items are from throughout Greece and Asia Minor. ⏱ *30 min. See p 62.*

❼ ★★ **Monastiraki Square.** The Tzisdarakis Tzami is the most prominent landmark on this animated square named for a small church known as the Little Monastery—all that remains of a monastic complex founded in the 10th century. The more distant past comes into view just to the south, where a columned wall of Hadrian's Library (p 32) suggests the grandeur of the sumptuous forum that the Roman Emperor built for learning and relaxation in A.D. 132. A 21st-century innovation is a glass enclosure revealing the Iridanos River, which once flowed freely around the base of the Acropolis and was considered by ancient Athenians to be sacred. ⏱ *10 min. Ermou and Athinas sts.*

❽ ★ **Abyssinia Square.** Monastiraki lives up to its reputation for

Adrianou Street.

bargain hunting along **Ifestou Street,** a narrow lane lined with shops selling tacky souvenirs and second-hand knickknacks. The environs are especially lively on Sunday mornings, when a flea market sets up in Abyssinia Square and the surrounding streets; some worthy antiques can be unearthed, but the mounds of vintage clothing and old housewares make it clear why the square is also known as Paliatzidika (the "secondhand-shop district"). 🕐 *15 min. Ermou, Normanou & Kinetou sts.*

⑨ ★★ Adrianou Street. The neighborhood's most pleasant street follows the north side of the Ancient Agora toward Kerameikos. Many of the 19th-century houses have been converted to cafes, so take a seat on one of the terraces and soak in the views over the ruins to the Acropolis. 🕐 *30 min.*

⑩ ★★ Kerameikos. The most important burying ground of ancient Athens, with many marble monuments still in place, exudes an aura of reverence. This green expanse of ruins was also a quarter for potters, a busy crossroads, and a popular gathering spot. Celebrants of the Eleusinian mysteries followed the Iera Odos (the "Sacred Way") through the Sacred Gate in Kerameikos to Demeter's temple in ancient Eleusis (now modern Elefsina, 22km/14 miles west); sections of the gate and road remain, as do segments of the 5th-century-B.C. "Long Walls" that provided a corridor from Athens to the sea at Piraeus. Noble Athenians gathered at the Diplyon Gate in Kerameikos to collect meat from the 100 cows slaughtered for the annual Panathenaic Festival, and travelers passed through the portal on their way in and out of the city. Kerameikos is one of the lesser-known ancient sites in Athens, so you can wander through these peaceful and storied surroundings at leisure. 🕐 *1 hr. See p 34.*

⑪ ★★ Technopolis. A former gasworks is now a hip arts complex that launched the surrounding Gazi neighborhood into trendiness. Furnaces and other industrial equipment remain in place, interspersed with art exhibits and performance spaces; one quiet corner pays homage to the great Greek-American diva Maria Callas. 🕐 *30 min. See p 15.*

The Technopolis.

The **Plaka** to **Psyrri**

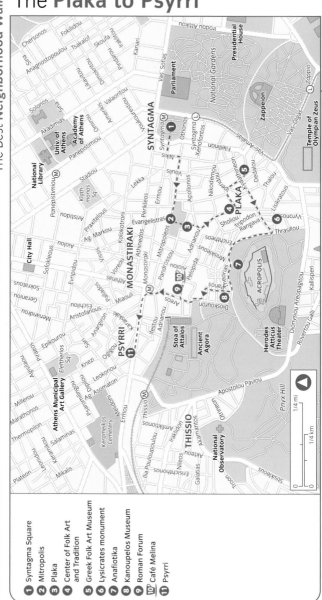

1 Syntagma Square
2 Mitropolis
3 Plaka
4 Center of Folk Art and Tradition
5 Greek Folk Art Museum
6 Lysicrates monument
7 Anafiotika
8 Kanoupelos Museum
9 Roman Forum
10 Café Melina
11 Psyrri

The Plaka, in the shadow of the Acropolis, is the heart of 19th-century Athens and well endowed with charm. Busy as the narrow streets can be, you'll come across many quiet corners, too, and a walk through the Plaka is never less than exhilarating. In Psyrri, just to the north, you'll discover the trendy side of Athens, as the old neighborhood of workshops and warehouses is being transformed into the city's favorite nighttime haunt. START: **Metro to Syntagma.**

A hand-painted doorway of a kafeneion (cafe) in Plaka is emblazoned with the current and past Greek flag.

1 ★★ **Syntagma Square.** Your starting point is the city's central square, at the northeast edge of Plaka. Mitropolis St. runs along the south side of Syntagma; follow it west to the eponymous cathedral. ⏱ *15 min. See p 13.*

2 ★ **Mitropolis.** The city's cathedral is home church to the archbishop of Athens and the chosen place of worship for the Athenian elite. Completed in 1862 amid the new capital's building boom, the massive walls incorporate marble from dozens of earlier churches

around the city that were demolished to make room for roads and buildings. Among the medieval landmarks that survived is Little Mitropolis, a tiny, exquisite 12th-century chapel next door that far out-charms its formidable neighbor. ⏱ *10 min.*

3 ★★★ kids **Plaka.** The most appealing quarter of central Athens is a warren of narrow lanes lined with 19th-century houses, interspersed here and there with medieval churches and ancient ruins. The charms of the quaint streets and shady squares are not lost on hordes of Athenians and their visitors who crowd shops, tavernas, and night spots. Even so, in your wanderings through the Plaka, you will come upon many peaceful corners and rewarding sights. ⏱ *1 hr. See p 10.*

4 ★ **Center of Folk Art and Tradition.** A walk south through the Plaka along shop-lined busy Adrianou Street brings you to the distinctive 1920s home of folklore scholar Angelika Hatzimichali (1895–1965). The wood-carved interior shows off the ceramics, embroideries, household items, and other pieces that Hatzimichali collected from throughout Greece in her pursuit of the folklore traditions that were in peril as 20th-century modernity swept over Greece. ⏱ *30 min. Hatzimichali and Geronta sts.* ☎ *210/324-3987. Free admission. Sept–July Mon–Sat 9am–1pm and 5–9pm.*

Despite crowds of shoppers, the narrow lanes of Plaka retain some small-village charm.

5 ★★ Folk Art Museum. Stop for a look at one of Greece's finest collections of tools, textiles, and traditional costumes—and don't miss the wonderful frescoed landscapes of Theophilos Hatzimichalis, a naïve artist who lived and worked on the island of Lesbos. To see more folk artistry, ask about the museum's several outposts in and around the Plaka, including the city's last Turkish *hamam*. ⏱ *1 hr. See p 42.*

6 ★ Lysicrates monument. Many so-called choragic monuments like this one once lined ancient Tripodon Street (Street of the Tripods, which still runs through Plaka). Choragics were producers who paid to train and costume choruses and dancers for festivals; winners displayed their trophies (three-footed vessels known as tripods) atop lavish monuments, of which only the one Lysicrates erected to show off the trophy he was awarded in the Dionysian festival of 334 B.C. remains. In the 1820s, Lord Byron wrote part of "Childe Harold" while staying in the

17th-century Capuchin monastery, now destroyed, that once surrounded the monument. ⏱ *10 min. Lysikratous and Herefondos sts. Metro: Akropoli.*

7 ★★ Anafiotika. The white-washed, stepped streets and bougainvillea clad houses of this quiet enclave climb the rocky slopes of the Acropolis. A world removed

A sidewalk cafe in front of the ruins of the Roman Agora.

from modern Athens, Anafiotiika was settled by masons and other craftsmen who migrated from Anafi and other Cycladic islands in the middle of the 19th century to find work building the new capital. They put up these simple houses by hand in the style of their homeland and also renovated the enchanting little 17th-century church of Agios Girogios tou Vrachou (St. George of the Cliff), perched on the flanks of the Acropolis Hill; in the garden is a memorial to Konstantinos Koukidos, an Acropolis guard who wrapped himself in a Greek flag and threw himself off the top of the bluff when the Germans invaded in 1941. 🕐 *30 min. See p 4.*

8 ★★ **Kanoupelos Museum.** Step into the handsome rooms of a neoclassical mansion for a leisurely perusal of a small but exquisite collection of antiquities, icons, jewelry, and other artifacts that cover the span of Greek artistry. 🕐 *30 min.*

9 ★★ **Roman Forum.** The western edge of the Plaka skirts the Roman Forum, the "new" agora funded and built by Julius Caesar in 51 B.C. when the Ancient Agora became too crowded. Much of the vast complex of shops and arcades remains buried, but several distinctive landmarks still rise from the ruins: the Tower of the Winds, a Roman era marble clock tower that incorporated sundials and a water clock; the main Athena Archegetis ("Athena the Leader") Gate, from around 11 B.C.; and the beautiful Fetiye mosque, an Ottoman addition from 1458. 🕐 *1 hr. See p 20.*

10 🍴 **Café Melina.** The favorite cafe of actress, political activist, and culture minister Melina Mecouri is now

Traditional briki (Greek coffee pots), like these for sale in Psyrri, allow for the proper amount of foam in your Greek coffee.

a shrine to her memory, where you can linger over coffee while listening to her music. *22 Lysiou St.* ☎ *210/324-6501. $.*

11 ★★★ **Psyrri.** Continue into Psyrri, by day a busy working-class neighborhood where leather crafters, tinsmiths, and basket weavers work out of small shops. When the sun sets, Psyrri transforms itself into Athens's prime showcase for night life, and nocturnal-by-nature Athenians crowd the tavernas, bars, and clubs until dawn. British poet Lord Byron, an ardent Philhellene who fought in the Greek War of Independence, boarded at 11 Agias Theklas St. (now a warehouse) in 1809. His landlord's 12-year-old daughter, Teresa Makris, inspired his poem "Maid of Athens." 🕐 *1 hr. See p 17.*

Kolonaki & Lycabettus

1 Numismatic Museum
2 Museum of Cycladic Art
3 Benaki Museum
4 Kolonaki Square
5 Lycabettus Hill
6 Orizontes

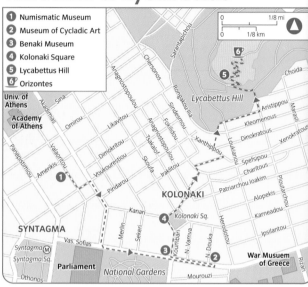

Athenians who are especially well coiffed, shod, and clothed tend to gravitate to Kolonaki. You may want to follow in their footsteps—not just to sip coffee in their favorite lairs, but to spend an afternoon stepping in and out of some of the city's finest museums, window-shopping in chic boutiques, and topping off the experience with an ascent to the top of Mt. Lycabettus for a spectacular view of the sun setting over the city. START: **Metro to Syntagma.**

1 ★★ **Numismatic Museum.** Even if you're not in the mood to hunch over the hoard of rare coins on display, at least take a good look at the mansion housing them. Ernst Ziller, a German architect King Otto imported to rebuild his new capital, designed this fascinating house just north of Syntagma Square in his telltale neoclassical style for Heinrich Schliemann, the archaeologist who famously excavated Troy and Mycenae (p 46). The house is fittingly known as the Iliou Melathron, or Ilium Mansion—Ilium is an ancient name for Troy. ⏱ **15 min.**

2 ★★★ **Museum of Cycladic Art.** Step into this stately mansion, another mid-19th-century landmark designed by Ernst Ziller, to admire the enigmatic figures left behind by the Cycladic civilization. The elongated marbles are hauntingly modern and, abstract as they are, touchingly human. ⏱ **1 hr. See p 37.**

3 ★★★ **Benaki Museum.** Stroll through the 36 rooms of the former home of the fabulously wealthy Benaki clan and stop to admire whatever it is that catches your eye—it might be a prehistoric tool, a piece of Byzantine jewelry, or

Sunset at the cafe atop Lycabettus Hill.

even an entire sumptuous room, transported here from Macedonia. ⏲ *1 hr. See p 37.*

④ ★ **Kolonaki Square.** The official name of the hub of the attractive Kolonaki district is Plateia Filikis Etairias ("Friendly Society"), an apt description for the scene that unfolds at the many outdoor cafes surrounding the patch of greenery. A well-heeled crowd

The wealthy, chic Kolonaki neighborhood of Athens.

keeps Athens's prime venue for *flaneurs* and society ladies hopping from early morning well into the wee hours. You will feel like an outsider if you're not toting a shopping bag or two from one of the many chic boutiques on the streets leading off the square. ⏲ *30 min. See p 13.*

⑤ ★★ **Lycabettus Hill.** One of the best shows in town is the spectacle of the sun setting over the city from atop the highest hill in Athens, with the Acropolis and the Saronic Gulf shimmering in the last light of the day. Should you be in need of exercise, climb to the top of the well-marked paths; otherwise, board the Teleferik (funicular) for the ascent. You may want to sip a coffee at the cafe before descending to the city spread out at your feet. ⏲ *1 hr. See p 13.*

⑥ ★ **Orizontes.** Should you not be able to tear yourself away from the view, take a seat on the sky-high terrace (a fair description of the prices, too). You may want to call ahead to ensure you get a table, since it's popular with romantically inclined couples. *Mt. Lycabettus.* ☎ *210/721-0701. $$$.*

Omonia & Exarchia

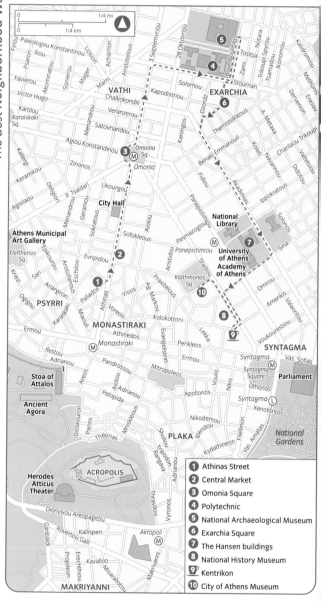

1. Athinas Street
2. Central Market
3. Omonia Square
4. Polytechnic
5. National Archaeological Museum
6. Exarchia Square
7. The Hansen buildings
8. National History Museum
9. Kentrikon
10. City of Athens Museum

Much of life in Athens transpires on and around busy and gritty **Omonia Square,** north of the Plaka. There's plenty to see—the central market, university, and National Archaeological Museum are all within easy reach—and you'll find no shortage of bustle and color. START: **Metro to Monastiraki.**

Omonia Square.

1 ★ **Athinas Street.** You can follow a pedestrian walkway, Aiolou, north to Omonia, but walk at least part of the way along this busy workaday avenue. Little shops cater to everyday needs, selling everything from tools and twine to votive candles and live chickens. ⏱ *15 min. Athinas St.*

2 ★★ **Central Market.** Just follow your nose to Athens's vast marketplace. Begin with a walk through the open-air stalls, then make your way past piles of fish, olives, and produce in the main hall. Cheese and plenty of other portable cornestibles are on hand, or you may want to take a seat at one of the many counters that serve tripe soup. ⏱ *30 min. Athinas St. See p 81.*

3 ★ **Omonia Square.** Another one of the city's hubs lacks the grace of Syntagma Square, surrounded as it is by a swirl of traffic and banal office blocks and frequented by some decidedly shady denizens. The everyday aspect of the space is not out of keeping with the square's history—when created as part of the renewal of the new capital in 1833, the square was intended to honor King Otto; after the unpopular monarch's ouster it became a hotbed of popular unrest and was renamed Omonia, which means Unity. ⏱ *10 min. Athinas and Konstantinou sts.*

4 ★ **Polytechnic.** The student uprisings of November 17, 1973, which toppled Greece's military junta and ushered in a new era of democracy, began in front of what is officially known as the National Technical University of Athens. Tanks moved in to crush the demonstrators, killing dozens; the fallen are memorialized by a marble statue of a youth, lying on the ground. ⏱ *10 min. Leoforos Eleftheriou Venezelou 46.*

5 ★★★ **National Archaeological Museum.** Artifacts from sights throughout Greece fill hall after hall to provide one of the world's great museum-going experiences—a mesmerizing look at many of the masterpieces of the ancient world, from Minoan frescoes to Mycenaean gold to classic statuary. ⏱ 2 hr. *See p 38.*

6 ★ **Exarchia Square.** The heart of the university district is surrounded by boho shops and laid-back, shabby chic cafes; join their black-clad ranks for a vicarious look at Athenian student and intellectual life. ⏱ *10 min. Stounari and Themistokeleous sts.*

7 ★★ **The Hansen buildings.** A trio of neoclassical landmarks by Theopolis and Christian Hansen—the Academy of Athens, the Senate of the University of Athens, and the National Library (p 47)—top the roster of edifices with which northern European architects graced Athens in the mid- to late 19th-century. The three marble extravaganzas may make you wish that plans to rebuild Athens as a grand European capital had come more fully to fruition. *See p 46–47.*

8 **National History Museum.** Collections surrounding the assembly hall of the *Palaia Vouli,* or Old Parliament (used 1875–1935) focus on "modern" Greek history, from the arrival of the Ottomans in the 15th century to World War II. ⏱ *30–45 min.*

A statue of Kapodistrias, first president of the modern college, greets visitors to the University of Athens.

The student quarter of Exarchia has long inspired revolutionary zeal and exuberant graffiti.

9 **Kentrikon.** This old-fashioned, lunch-only (Mon–Sat noon–6pm) spot under a shopping arcade across from the History Museum is a favorite with shoppers and office workers, who value the good food and unpretentious service. *3 Kolokotroni St.* ☎ *210/323-2482. $.*

10 **City of Athens Museum.** Should you have time and energy for one more stop, step into the modest 1830s house where King Otto and Queen Amalia set up temporary housekeeping while their royal palace (now Parliament) was being built. The reception rooms, study, and library are set up to look like the royal couple, still teenagers when they came to Athens, might pop in at any moment, and, most intriguingly, a plaster model to the scale of 1:1,000 shows what the city looked like in 1872, when it was home to just 25,000 souls. ⏱ *30–45 min. 7 Paparigopoulou St.* ☎ *210/323-1397. Admission 3€, 2€ seniors and students. www. athenscitymuseum.gr. Mon & Wed–Fri 9am–4pm; Sat–Sun 10am–3pm.* ●

Shopping **Best Bets**

Best **Folk Art**
★ Amorgos, *3 Kodrou St. (p 77)*

Best Place to Study **Contemporary Greek Art**
★★ Astrolavos-Dexameni, *11 Xanthippou St. (p 73)*

Best **Spice & Herb Shop**
★ Bahar, *31 Evripidou St. (p 76)*

Best **Museum Reproduction Gifts**
★ Benaki Museum Gift Shop, *1 Koumbari St. (p 77)*

Best **Bookstore**
★ Eleftheroudakis, *17 Panepistimiou St. (p 74)*

Best **Sunday Flea Market**
★ Gazi Flea Market, *Ermou & Pareos sts. (p 81)*

Best **Food Shopping**
★★★ Central Market, *Athinas St. (p 81)*

Best Place for **Designer Shoes**
★ Kalogirou, *4 Patriarchou Ioakim St. (p 82)*

Best Source for **Sandals**
★★★ Stavros Melissinos, *2 Agias Theklas St. (p 82)*

Best **Magazine Shop**
★ Kiosk, *18 Omonia Sq. (p 74)*

Best Place to **Satisfy a Sweet Tooth**
★ Karavan, *11 Voukourestiou St. (p 76)*

Best Place for **Skincare Products**
★ Korres, *8 Ivikou St. (p 74)*

Best Known **Athenian Jeweler**
★ Lalaounis, *6 Panepistimiou St. (p 80)*

Best Place for **Traditional Greek Coffees**
★ Loumidis, *106 Aiolou St. (p 77)*

Best Place for **Worry Beads**
★ Mala (Komboloi Club), *1 Praxitelous St. (p 78)*

Best Selection of **Byzantine Jewelry**
★ Byzantino, *120 Adrianou St. (p 80)*

Best Place for **Musical Instruments**
★ Philippos Nakas Conservatory, *44 Panepistimiou St. (p 82)*

Best **One-Stop Souvenir Shopping**
★ Shopping Center Plaka, *1 Pandrossou St. (p 79)*

This page: Lalaounis recreates ancient and Byzantine jewelry. Previous page: A selection of ceramic chalices at the Sunday flea market in Monastiraki.

Monastiraki, Plaka & Omonia
Shopping

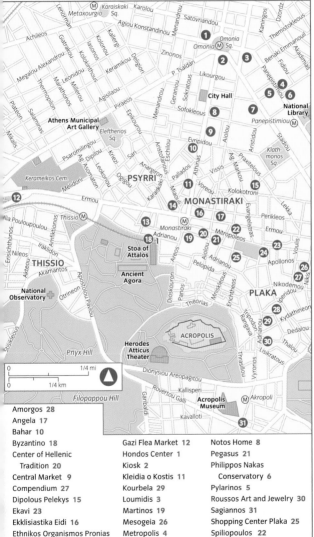

Syntagma & Kolonaki Shopping

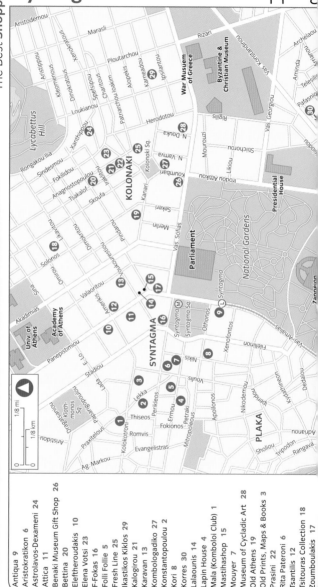

Athens Shopping A to Z

Antique guns, first-edition books, and prints for sale at Antiqua, which also sells old coins, swords, icons, and so on.

Antiques & Collectibles

Antiqua SYNTAGMA   One of Athens's oldest and finest antiques dealers sells 19th-century watercolors, icons, coins, and other easy-to-carry high-end souvenirs. *2 Amalias Ave.* ☎ *210/323-2220. www.antiqua.gr. AE, DC, MC, V. Metro: Syntagma. Map p 72.*

Kleidia o Kostis PSYRRI   If you have a goat at home, you'll find the perfect accoutrement—and one of these quaint handmade goat bells is sure to be a conversation piece even if you are goat-less. *17 Athinas St.* ☎ *210/321-0442. No credit cards. Metro: Monastiraki. Map p 71.*

★★ Martinos MONASTIRAKI   One of the city's most esteemed dealers sells only the finest furniture, along with such collectibles as rare Venetian glass, centuries-old silver, oil paintings, and intricately carved Byzantine-era doors. You'll also find a branch at 24 Pindarou St. in Kolanaki. *50 Pandrossou St.* ☎ *210/321-3110. AE, DC, MC, V. Metro: Monastiraki. Map p 71.*

Old Prints, Maps & Books SYN-TAGMA   The stock of old maps, books, and drawings here is extensive and includes some beautiful prints of flowers and birds. *15 Kolokotroni St.* ☎ *210/323-0923. www. oldprints.gr. AE, DC, MC, V. Metro: Syntagma or bus: 200. Map p 72.*

Pylarinos PLAKA   Old engravings of Athens share crowded shelf space with an amazing collection of old coins. *50 Panepistimiou St.* ☎ *210/363-0688. No credit cards. Metro: Syntagma. Map p 71.*

Art

★★ Astrolavos-Dexameni KOLONAKI   This highly touted gallery plays a big part in bringing attention to the Greek art scene, showing well-known and up-and-coming artists. Branches are in Kolonaki, at 11 Irodotou St. (☎ *210/722-1200*), as well as in Piraeus, at 140 Androutsou St. (☎ *210/412-8002*). *11 Xanthippou St.* ☎ *210/729-4342 or 210/729-4343. www.astrolavos.gr. AE, DC, MC, V. Metro: Syntagma. Map p 72.*

Ekklisiastika Eidi MONASTI-RAKI   A large showroom and workshop on the premises can supply an

Astrolavas-Dexameni shows the work of contemporary Greek artists (see p 73).

icon of any saint you'd like. *9 Agias Eirinis St.* ☎ *210/325-2047. AE, DC, V. Metro: Monastiraki. Map p 71.*

Ikastikos Kiklos KOLONAKI One of Athens's largest and sleekest galleries showcases contemporary Greek artists; there are a few Kiklos locations around the city. *20 Karneadou St.* ☎ *210/729-1642. www. ikastikos-kiklos.gr. AE, MC, V. Metro: Syntagma. Map p 72.*

Zoumboulakis SYNTAGMA Athens's oldest gallery has introduced the work of many Greek artists over the decades; the Syntagma store specializes in silkscreens, poster art, and ceramics, while a branch on Kolonaki Square shows original work as well as antiques. *26 Kriezoutou St.* ☎ *210/363-4454. www. zoumboulakis.gr. AE, MC, V. Metro: Syntagma. Map p 72.*

Beauty & Toiletries
Fresh Line KOLONAKI This shop's skin-care products and colorful rough-cut soaps are made from all-natural organically grown ingredients; many are based on ancient formulas. *10 Skoufa St.* ☎ *210/364-4015. www.freshline.gr. AE, MC, V. Metro: Syntagma. Map p 72.*

★ **Korres** PANGRATI These natural, environmentally friendly

skin-care products were concocted in this modest pharmacy and, now an international sensation, are also available at shops around Athens and the world. *8 Ivikou St. at Erathosthenous St.* ☎ *210/722-2774. www.korres.com. AE, DC, MC, V. Metro: Syntagma. Map p 72.*

Books & Magazines
Compendium PLAKA A small and friendly outlet for English-language titles, Compendium sells old and used books, along with a good selection of magazines. *28 Nikis St.* ☎ *210/322-1248. Metro:Syntagma. Map p 71.*

★ **Eleftheroudakis** SYNTAGMA Browse Athens's largest selection of English titles, with a huge selection of travel books, then pull up a seat in the pleasant cafe to linger over your selections. *17 Panepistimiou St.* ☎ *210/331-4480. www.books.gr. AE, DC, MC, V. Metro: Panepistimiou. Map p 72.*

★ **Kiosk** OMONIA Athens's best-stocked foreign-press *periptero* (kiosk) never closes, which is fortunate for news and magazine junkies.

Handmade-in-Greece body oils and creams on the shelves at Fresh Line.

Buyer Beware

Despite assurances from the shopkeeper, that rare icon you are getting for a bargain may be fresh out of the factory. While Athens has many reputable antiques and arts dealers, some souvenir dealers pass off freshly minted icons and wood carvings as antiques. If it's cheap, it's probably not genuine, and if a piece is genuine, you may require a special export license to take it out of the country. In general, this applies to all antiquities and to icons more than 100 years old, though not necessarily to coins and some jewelry. A reputable dealer will explain the ins and outs.

18 Omonia Sq. at Athinas St. ☎ 210/322-2402. No credit cards. Metro: Omonia. Map p 71.

Stoa tou Vivliou OMONIA   An entire shopping arcade is devoted to books—rare volumes, current editions (some in English), and rare bindings are a bibliophile's delight. 5 Pesmzoglou St. ☎ 210/325-3989. www.stoabibliou.gr. Metro: Omonia. Map p 71.

Department Stores

Attica SYNTAGMA   Up-and-coming Greek designers are among those showcased throughout eight floors of fashionable clothing, and the store also sells high-end furniture and housewares. 9 Panepistimiou St. ☎ 211/180-2500. www.atticadps.gr. AE, DC, MC, V. Metro: Syntagma. Map p 72.

F-Fokas PANEPISTIMIOU   The brand-name sports- and casual wear on sale here, including many lines for children, are from Greek and international designers. 41 Stadiou St. ☎ 210/325-7770. www.fokas.gr. AE, DC, MC, V. Metro: Syntagma. Map p 72.

Hondos Center OMONIA   The flagship store of this toiletries chain has all the grooming items you'll ever need, along with clothing for men

and women, kitchenware, linen luggage, and many other accessories for you and your home. Don't leave without checking out the lavish perfume counters or stopping on the top floor to enjoy the view of the city over coffee. 4 Omonia Sq. ☎ 210/528-2800. www.hondos.gr. AE, DC, MC, V. Metro: Omonia. Map p 71.

Notos Home OMONIA   Everything for the home, including fine crystal, fills eight floors of the Omonia outpost; if you're looking for clothing, cosmetics, and accessories, head to the Notos store in the Plaka at 99 Aiolou St. ☎ 210/324-5811.

Kiosk's multitude of Greek and foreign-press magazines and newspapers.

5 Kratinou St. at Kotzia Sq. ☎ 210/
374-3000. www.notoshome.gr. AE,
DC, MC, V. Metro: Omonia. Map
p 71.

Fashion

Bettina KOLONAKI   Several internationally known Greek designers
share rack space, showing off the
latest word in Greek fashion. *40 Pindarou & 29 Anagnostopoulou sts.*
☎ *210/339-2094. AE, DC, MC, V.
Metro: Syntagma or bus: 200.
Map p 72.*

★ **Kourbela** PLAKA   Comfy, rea-
sonably priced, and eco-friendly
linen-and-silk-and-cotton-blend uni-
sex clothing is offered alongside
Greek-made classic knits. *109 Adrianou St.* ☎ *210/322-4591. www.
ionnakourbela.com. AE, DC, MC, V.
Metro: Syntagma or Monastiraki.
Map p 71.*

Rita Pateroni SYNTAGMA
Lovely and well-priced clothing by
an Athenian designer is stylish and
distinctly Greek. *11 Karayioryi Servias St.* ☎ *210/322-7101. www.
ritapateroni.gr. DC, MC, V. Metro:
Syntagma. Map p 72.*

Dresses on sale at the boutique Bettina.

*A combination from Rita Pateroni, who
designs women's prêt-a-porter and tailor-
made garments.*

Tsantilis SYNTAGMA   A well-
known supplier of top-quality fabric
to the clothing trade sells distinctive
designs by the yard, as well as an
attractive and well-priced collection
of designer clothing. *6 Panepistimiou
St. at Voukourestiou St.* ☎ *210/360-
6815. www.tsantilis.gr. DC, MC, V.
Metro: Syntagma. Map p 72.*

Food & Wine

Aristokratikon SYNTAGMA
Athens's premiere purveyor of
chocolate has been turning out dec-
adently rich creations since 1928.
9 Karayioryi Servias St. ☎ *210/322-
0546. www.aristokratikon.com.
Metro: Syntagma. Map p 72.*

★ **Bahar** AGORA   Spices and dried
herbs from Greek mountainsides are
accompanied by herbal oils and
other elixirs; the bags of herbs and
mountain teas are ideal for easy-to-
carry gifts. *31 Evripidou St.* ☎ *210/
321-7225. www.bahar-spices.gr. No
credit cards. Metro: Omonia or
Monastiraki or bus: 025, 026, 027,
035, 049, 200, 227. Map p 71.*

★ **Karavan** SYNTAGMA   The
gooey-dessert deprived can sate

their cravings here; bite-sized, honey-soaked baklava and *kadaifi* (Greek pastry with nuts and syrup) are the specialties. *11 Voukourestiou St.* ☎ *210/364-1540. www. karavan.gr. No credit cards. Metro: Syntagma. Map p 72.*

★ **Loumidis** OMONIA   This old-fashioned coffee roaster has been around since 1920. You can choose from a huge variety of Greek and Turkish coffees and the *briki* (traditional little coffee pots) in which to brew them. *106 Aiolou St. at Panepistimiou St.* ☎ *210/321-6965. No credit cards. Metro: Omonia. Map p 71.*

Mastihashop SYNTAGMA   *Loukoumi* (Turkish Delight), intoxicating liqueurs, soaps, salves, gum, and all sorts of other products are made from mastic harvested on the island of Chios. *Panepistimiou & Kriezotou sts.* ☎ *210/363-2750. www.mastihashop.gr. AE, MC, V. Metro: Syntagma. Map p 72.*

Mesogeia PLAKA   One of the neighborhood's remaining traditional groceries sells cheeses, olive oil, ouzo, and other staples of Greek life. *52 Nikis St. MC, V. Metro: Syntagma. Map p 71.*

Gifts
★ **Amorgos** PLAKA   Wooden utensils, finely embroidered linens,

The Benaki Museum Gift Shop.

shadow puppets—anything Greek-made seems to find a place on the cramped shelves here. *3 Kodrou St.* ☎ *210/324-3836. AE, DC, MC, V. Metro: Syntagma. Map p 71.*

★ **Benaki Museum Gift Shop** KOLONAKI   The reproductions of gold and silver jewelry, textiles, and ceramics from the Benaki museum collections are exquisite. *1 Koumbari St. at Vas. Sofias Ave.* ☎ *210/ 367-1000. www.benaki.gr. AE, DC, MC, V. Map p 72.*

Center of Hellenic Tradition MONASTIRAKI   Genuine folk arts and crafts from around Greece,

Culinary herbs and spices in bags at Bahar.

Backgammon or tavli boards, like these from Ekavi, are a common pastime in Greek cafes.

including pottery, decorative roof tiles, and old-fashioned painted-wood shop signs, are on offer, as is delicious light fare in the shop's cafe. *36 Pandrossou & 59 Mitropoleos sts.* ☎ *210/321-3023. AE, DC, MC, V. Metro: Monastiraki. Map p 71.*

Dipolous Pelekys PLAKA Pillow cases, bed linens, and blouses are embroidered by several generations of the family that lovingly runs this delightful shop. *Kolokotroni 3.* ☎ *210/322-3783. MC, V. Metro: Syntagma. Map p 71.*

A selection of silverware from Konstantopoulou.

★ **Ekavi** MONASTIRAKI *Tavli* (backgammon) sets—the game of choice for Greece's *kafeneion* (cafe) crowd—and chess sets with pieces resembling Olympic athletes and Greek gods are handmade by the Manopoulos workshops in wood, metal, or stone. *36 Mitropoleos St.* ☎ *210/323-7740. www.manopoulos. com. AE, DC, MC, V. Metro: Monastiraki or Syntagma or bus: 025, 026, 027. Map p 71.*

★ **Ethnikos Organismos Pronias (National Welfare Organization)** PLAKA Traditional Greek designs include rugs, tapestries, and beautifully embroidered linens made by disadvantaged women around the country. Prices start at 20€ for a small embroidery. *6 Ypatias St.* ☎ *210/325-0524. AE, DC, MC, V. Metro: Syntagma. Map p 71.*

Kombologadiko KOLONAKI *Komboloi* ("worry" beads) are fashioned from bone, stone, wood, and antique amber—and can be worn as jewelry as well as used as a stress reliever. *6 Koumbari St.* ☎ *212/700-0090. www.kombologadiko.gr. AE, DC, MC, V. Metro: Syntagma. Map p 72.*

Konstantopoulou SYNTAGMA Lekka Street is one long row of silver shops; Konstantopoulou carries the largest selection of table settings, candlesticks, cutlery, and the like. *23 Lekka St.* ☎ *210/322-7997. AE, DC, MC, V. Metro: Syntagma. Map p 72.*

Kori SYNTAGMA An eclectic selection of pottery, folk pieces, and reproductions of antiquities—many by up-and-coming Greek artists—put a new twist on the concept of souvenirs. *13 Mitropoleos St.* ☎ *210/323-3534. AE, DC, MC, V. Metro: Syntagma. Map p 72.*

★ **Mala (Komboloi Club)** SYNTAGMA Beautiful amber worry

Roussos Art and Jewelry sells homemade bronze statuettes of the Greek gods.

beads are the house specialty, though *komboloi* fashioned from many other materials are also available; prices run from 15€ to 9,000€. *1 Praxitelous St.* ☎ *210/331-0145. www.komboloiclub.com. MC, V. Metro: Panepistimiou. Map p 72.*

★ **Museum of Cycladic Art**
KOLONAKI   The reproductions of Cycladic figurines from the museum's collection are beautiful, as is the jewelry fashioned on ancient and Byzantine pieces. *4 N. Douka St. at Vas. Sofias Ave.* ☎ *210/722-8321 or 210/722-8323. www.cycladic.gr.*

Closed Tues & Sun. AE, DC, MC, V. Metro: Syntagma. Map p 72.

Roussos Art and Jewelry
PLAKA   This store's porcelain dolls, dressed in traditional costumes, are made at a workshop in western Athens; prices start at about 40€. Other handcrafted Greek-made trinkets are also available. *121 Adrianou St. at Kydathineon St.* ☎ *210/322-6395. Metro: Akropoli. Map p 71.*

★ **Shopping Center Plaka**
MONASTIRAKI   Do all your souvenir shopping in one go on three crammed levels. A standout is the

A Tradition of Craftsmanship

Greeks have been mastering fine craftsmanship for millennia, and the tradition is very much alive today. Most noticeably, you'll come across excellent workmanship in the leather goods (Greek shoes and sandals are especially well crafted) and gold and silver jewelry (Byzantine reproductions are elaborate and appealing) that fill shop windows around Athens. You may also want to partake of some age-old traditions and equip yourself with beautiful handwoven textiles, a strand of exquisite *komboli* (worry beads), ceramics (you can find some exquisite new versions of the black-and-red pottery the ancients perfected), or a *tavli* board, a staple of *kafenions* (coffeehouses). Whatever catches your eye, remember that bargaining is also a time-honored Greek tradition.

Where to Get It

Jewelry, shoes, and edibles are standouts on the Athens shopping scene. Kolonaki is the **upmarket designer clothing** district, while **shoes** and **chain stores** are on central Ermou Street, running off Syntagma Square. Adrianou Street in Plaka, down to Pandrossou Street in Monastiraki, is prime turf for **souvenirs** and **jewelry.** Shops specializing in **made-in-Greece goods** are concentrated around Athinas Street in Monastiraki and in parts of the Plaka—you'll find **textiles** along Athinaidos Street and **church-related supplies** on Apollonos Street near the Mitropoleos cathedral. Abyssinia Square in Monastiraki hosts the city's largest **flea market** and many of the surrounding shops sell **used and antique furniture.** For **hip and cool** items, head to the streets around youth-oriented Exarchia Square, or Ifestou Street in Monastiraki. Be wary that Athens's street names may change by the block (Adrianou, for example) and spellings can vary considerably, so keep a good map at hand.

writing paper, with Greek motifs. *1 Pandrossou St.* ☎ *210/324-5405. www.shoppingplaka.com. AE, MC, V. Metro: Monastiraki. Map p 71.*

Tsitouras Collection KOLONAKI   Understated design and high quality are the hallmarks of this line of distinguished housewares—including fine crystal and silver. The house also makes beautiful scarves and ties. *80 Solonos St.* ☎ *210/362-2326. www.tsitouras.com. AE, MC, V. Metro: Panepistimo. Map p 72.*

Jewelry

★ **Byzantino** PLAKA   Many of Byzantino's gold pieces are replicas of ancient and Byzantine jewelry, and the shop also creates beautiful original designs. *120 Adrianou St.* ☎ *210/324-6605. www.byzantino.com. Metro: Monastiraki. Map p 71.*

Elena Votsi KOLONAKI   The designer's larger-than-life creations in coral and semiprecious stones make quite a statement—and are popular with celebs and fashionistas around the world. *7 Xanthou St.*

☎ *210/360-0936. www.elenavotsi. com. Metro: Syntagma. Map p 72.*

Folli Follie SYNTAGMA   The trendy costume jewelry, watches, and accessories in gold and silver from this international chain are appealing and affordable. *18 Ermou St.* ☎ *210/323-0729. www.follifollie.gr. AE, DC, MC, V. Metro: Syntagma. Map p 72.*

Browsing at the Gazi Flea Market.

★ **Lalaounis** SYNTAGMA   One of Greece's best-known jewelers crafts exquisite gold and silver pieces based on ancient and Byzantine designs. Even if you're not in the market to buy, pay a visit to the wonderful museum housed in the old Lalaounis workshops (p 41). *6 Panepistimiou St. at Voukourestiou St.* ☎ *210/361-1371. Museum: 12 Karyatidon St., Makriyanni.* ☎ *210/922-1044. www.lalaounis-jewelry museum.gr. AE, DC, MC, V. Metro: Syntagma. Map p 72.*

★ **Sagiannos** ACROPOLIS   This inventive designer is such an institution that there is no sign in front of his stylish shop. Recent designs feature bar codes and other contemporary elements, though simple spheres are the designer's trademark. *3 Makriyanni.* ☎ *210/924-7323. AE, DC, MC, V. Metro: Acropolis. Map p 71.*

Kids

kids **Angela** MONASTIRAKI Parents-to-be will be delighted with traditional baptism or christening clothes and related items, including *boubouniera* (baptism favors). *9 Kalamiotou St. at Kapnikareas St.* ☎ *210/323-8448. www.angela.gr. Metro: Monastiraki. Map p 71.*

A girl's shoe from the esteemed Greek brand name Mouyer.

kids **Lapin House** SYNTAGMA This Greek chain offers nice, high-quality kid's clothes, at prices that relegate them to the Sunday best category. *21 Ermou St.* ☎ *210/324-1316. www.lapinhouse.com. AE, DC, MC, V. Metro: Syntagma. Map p 72.*

kids **Mouyer** SYNTAGMA   Re-shod your footsore young traveling companions at this century-old purveyor of sturdy children's shoes. *6 Ermou St.* ☎ *210/323-2831. www.mouyer. gr. AE, DC, MC, V. Metro: Syntagma. Map p 72.*

Markets

★★★ **Central Market** OMONIA Farmers' markets appear once a week in neighborhoods around the city, but the daily (except Sun) Varvakio Agora is the place to go—a visual, aural, and olfactory slap in the face that will introduce you to many things you never knew people ate. *Athinas St. at Sofokleous St. Mon–Thurs 6am–3pm; Fri–Sat 6am–6pm. Metro: Omonia or Monastiraki or bus: 025, 026, 035, 049, 100, 200, 227, 400. Map p 71.*

★ **Gazi Flea Market** GAZI   You'll have to shift through piles of junk, but you can score some good finds, and prices are often lower than they are at the better known flea market in Monastiraki. Beware of pickpockets as you browse. *Ermou & Piraeus sts. Sun early morning to 3 or 4pm. Metro: Thissio or Kerameikos. Map p 71.*

Monastiraki Flea Market MONASTIRAKI   Trinket and artifacts shops crowd the narrow alleys of Monastiraki, particularly along Pandrossou and Ifestou streets. The "official" flea market is the one held in Abyssinia Square since 1910. You'll find dusty books, military uniforms, coins and stamps, light fixtures, plates, cutlery, furniture—just about anything, really. *Abyssinia Sq. at Ermou, Normanou & Kinetou sts. Daily 9am–9pm; best on Sun. Metro: Monastiraki. Map p 71.*

Musical instruments are sold at Philippos Nakas Conservatory.

Music

Metropolis OMONIA   The city's best known source for recorded music is also a big outlet for concert and event tickets. Greek music is sold at the no. 54 address, with its distinctive wrought-iron overhang; no. 64 sells both foreign and Greek titles. *54 & 64 Panepistimiou St.* ☎ *210/361-1463. AE, DC, MC, V. Metro: Omonia. Map p 71.*

Pegasus MONASTIRAKI   The *bouzouki* instruments, stringed *tabouras* (a type of lute), and small hand-held "bongo" *touberlekia* drums sold here are all handmade. *26 Pandrossou St.* ☎ *210/324-2036. 92 Adrianou St.* ☎ *210/324-2601. www.pegasus greece.com. AE, DC, MC, V. Metro: Monastiraki. Map p 71.*

★ **Philippos Nakas Conservatory** OMONIA   The city's favorite music store sells instruments, from *bouzoukis* to electric guitars, sheet music, and all sorts of related gadgetry for serious musicians. *44*

Panepistimiou St. ☎ *210/361-2720. www.nakas.gr. AE, DC, MC, V. Metro: Panepistimiou. Map p 71.*

Shoes

★ **Kalogirou** KOLONAKI   Four floors of an old mansion are filled with designer shoes; you'll also find a good selection in less atmospheric surroundings in the Plaka. *4 Patriarchou Ioakim St.* ☎ *210/722-8804. Plaka: 12 Pandrossou St.* ☎ *210/331-0727. www.lemonis.gr. AE, DC, MC, V. Metro: Syntagma or bus for Kolonaki branch: 022, 060, 200. Map p 72.*

★★ **Old Athens** KOLONAKI   All the shoes here are made in Greece, and they are jaw-droppingly beautiful, classy, and chic. *17 Kanari St.* ☎ *210/361-4762. AE, DC, MC, V. Metro: Syntagma. Map p 72.*

Prasini KOLONAKI   Fashionistas flock to this elegant shop that sells top European designs as well as designer-name bags. *7–9 Tsakalof St.* ☎ *210/364-6258. AE, DC, MC, V. Metro: Syntagma. Map p 72.*

Spiliopoulos MONASTIRAKI   These designer shoes at bargain prices are "seconds" that never made it past quality control, but who could find the flaw? Be prepared to fight for bench space. Bags, wallets, and purses are also stocked. *63 Ermou St.* ☎ *210/322-7590. AE, MC, V. 50 Adrianou St.* ☎ *210/321-9096. DC, MC, V. Metro: Monastiraki. Map p 71.*

★★★ **Stavros Melissinos** PSYRRI   Sophia Loren, Jackie O., and Anthony Quinn are among the international roster of celebs who have sported the house's trademark, hand-made leather sandals, first created in 1954. The son of the famous Stavros, known as the "poet shoemaker," now runs the enterprise. *2 Agias Theklas St.* ☎ *210/321-9247. www.melissinos-poet.com. No credit cards. Metro: Monastiraki. Map p 71.* ●

5 The Great **Outdoors**

The Best of **Green Athens**

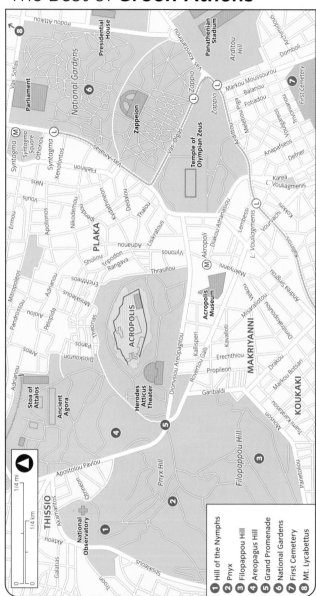

1 Hill of the Nymphs
2 Pnyx
3 Filopappou Hill
4 Areopagus Hill
5 Grand Promenade
6 National Gardens
7 First Cemetery
8 Mt. Lycabettus

Previous page: The port at Perdika, Aegina.

Athens is surprisingly graced with a generous amount of greenery. The pine-covered hills in central Athens—Filopappou, Pnyx, and the Hill of the Nymphs—Mt. Lycabettus across town, the National Gardens, and even a cemetery offer easy-to-get-to escapes. Some of these retreats offer superb views—of the city, the Parthenon, and the Saronic Gulf—and all provide a nice sense of relaxation.
START: **Metro to Thissio, or walk from the Acropolis or Plaka.**

① Hill of the Nymphs. The northernmost of the hills surrounding the Acropolis is topped by the **National Observatory,** built in 1842 according to designs by Theophilos Hansen, the Danish architect of the Academy at the University of Athens (see p 47) and many other public buildings around the capital. Just below is the multi-domed **Agia Marina** church, a 20th-century replacement of an earlier church honoring Saint Marina, the patron saint of childbirth. Her presence here continues the hill's long association with nymphs who were believed to protect pregnant women and sick children. Ancient Athenians would leave the garments of sick children beneath the trees in the hopes that nymphs would work a cure. In places the rugged hillsides are etched with caves, including one known as the **Prison of Socrates** and said to be where the philosopher was held and forced to drink hemlock after being found guilty of corrupting Athenian youth; the story is unproven and highly unlikely but adds a bit of romance to the bucolic surroundings. Also adding to the rural prospect of the hillside are a herd of white ponies used to pull horse and buggies on the tourist route and brought here to graze during off-hours. *Dionysiou Areopagitou/Apostolou Pavlou sts.*

② Pnyx. The ancient **Assembly** met on the Pnyx during the 5th and 4th centuries B.C., which more or less makes the hilltop the birthplace of democracy. Any citizen of Athens was welcome to come here to debate and vote on matters of importance to the city. Granted, women were not allowed to be citizens, and most residents of the city were slaves. Even so, it's chilling to think that Pericles stood on this spot to argue for funds to build the Parthenon—which would prove to be such a distraction that in 404 B.C.

The Agia Marina church was built on the site of an older church on the Hill of the Nymphs in 1922; the National Observatory is in the background.

Filopappou Hill is a rejuvenating perch for a quick retreat from the city below.

the semicircle of benches on which the Assembly convened was turned around so the display of glowing marble was at the members' backs. Take a seat and gaze across to the Acropolis to see just how engaging the spectacle of the monument still is. *Dionysiou Areopagitou/Apostolou Pavlou sts.*

3 ★ **Filopappou Hill.** The adjoining Filopappou Hill (often called Hill of the Muses) is topped by the **Filopappou Monument,** a marble tomb erected in A.D. 116 in honor of the Roman consul of Athens, Julius Antiochus Philopappus. It was from this vantage point that the Venetians bombed the Parthenon in 1687—these days eager shutterbugs gather to take advantage of the unobstructed sight lines to snap pictures of the monument. Paths meander over the hill, leading to the Byzantine church of **Ayios Demetrios** and the **Dora Stratou Theatre,** where the renowned folk dancing troupe performs on summer evenings (p 128). ⏱ *1 hr. Dionysiou Areopagitou/Apostolou Pavlou sts.*

4 ★ **Areopagus Hill.** This bald granite peak next to the Acropolis is ascended by steep stairs carved out of the rock. The climb didn't deter noble Athenians from convening on the summit to try cases of homicide, or the followers of St. Paul from gathering to listen to the apostle preach

Christianity. Provided the steps are not treacherously rain-slick, make the climb for knockout views of the Parthenon and other monuments on the Acropolis—they are right at eye level from this vantage point and so close you can almost reach out and touch them. *Dionysiou Areopagitou/Apostolou Pavlou sts.*

5 ★★★ **Grand Promenade.** Walking along this cobblestone-and-marble, pedestrians-only boulevard that skirts Acropolis Hill is one of the capital's greatest pleasures—the great monuments of ancient Greece surround you, and the air is scented with pine. *See p 26.*

6 ★ **National Gardens.** These lawns, shaded paths, and ponds were once the park of the Royal Palace (now Parliament, see p 45) and since 1847 have been open to all, a welcome refuge in the busy city center. If you're up for a longer walk, continue south through more greenery—past the **Zappeion Hall,** a neoclassical hall built for the revival of the Olympic Games in the 1890s (p 45), and the **Temple of Olympian Zeus,** completed by Roman Emperor Hadrian in A.D. 132 (p 31). Just to the north you'll come to the First Cemetery.

7 ★ **First Cemetery.** Since the 19th century, prominent Athenians have been laid to rest in this sprawling parklike expanse of greenery that climbs the cypress- and pine-clad slopes of Ardittos Hill behind the Temple of Olympian Zeus. Among those buried here are Heinrich Schliemann, the archaeologist who uncovered Troy and Mycenae, and Melina Mecouri, the actress, activist, and politician who launched the battle for the return of the Parthenon Frieze (p 28). Even some of the lesser known are laid to rest beneath spectacular monuments, many carved by stone masons from the island of Tinos. The cemetery's most beloved monument is *Sleeping Lady* (1877), crafted by Tiniot Yannoulis Halepas for the tomb of Sophia Afentaki, the 18-year-old daughter of a wealthy Athenian. Walking along the shaded lanes is a popular outing; many Athenians gather here to picnic near the graves of their loved ones. *Anapafseos & Trivonianou sts., Mets.* ☎ *210/923-6720. Apr–Oct 8am–8pm; Nov–Mar 8am–5:30pm. Bus: A3, A4, 057, 103, 108, 111, 155, 206, 208, 237, 856, or 227 (to A' "Proto" Nekrotafio).*

8 ★★★ **Mt. Lycabettus.** The highest hill in Athens, topped with the gleaming white **church of Ayios Giorgios,** is the city's favorite viewpoint. An early evening

Birds in flight at the National Gardens.

ascent via the funicular from Kolonaki usually ensures a breeze, a spectacular sunset to the west, and a moonrise to the east. Views extend as far as the island of Aegina, and Athens looks especially inviting from on high. Some of the gazers stay for drinks and dinner at Orizontes restaurant or the adjoining Cafe Lycabettus (p 106), but most are content with a soda and snack from one of the kiosks. You can walk down (or up, for that matter) on one of the many well-marked paths. *See p 13.*

Sleeping Lady, a monument in Athens's First Cemetery, depicts Sophia Afentaki, who died at age 18.

Rambling Around **Attica**

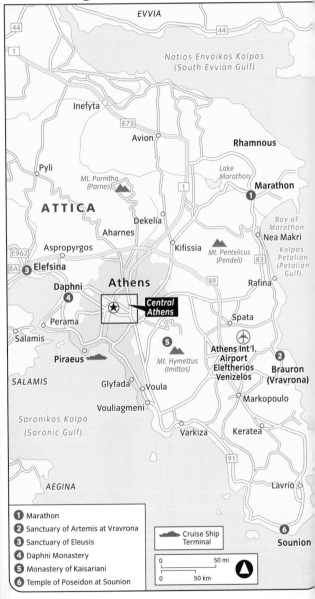

EVVIA

44

1

*Notios Envoikos Kolpos
(South Evvian Gulf)*

E75

Inefyta

Avion

Rhamnous

Pyli

*Mt. Parnitha
(Parnes)*

*Lake
Marathon*

Marathon ❶

ATTICA

Dekelia

1

*Bay of
Marathon*

Aharnes

Kifissia

Nea Makri

Aspropyrgos

*Mt. Pentelicus
(Pendeli)*

83

*Kolpos
Petalion
(Petalian
Gulf)*

E962

8A ❸ **Elefsina**

Daphni
❹

Athens

89

Rafina

Perama

Spata

Salamis

❺

Piraeus

*Mt. Hymettus
(Imittos)*

**Athens Int'l.
Airport
Eleftherios
Venizelos**

❷

**Brauron
(Vravrona)**

SALAMIS

Glyfada

Voula

Markopoulo

Vouliagmeni

*Saronikos Kolpo
(Saronic Gulf)*

Varkiza

Keratea

91

AEGINA

Lavrio

❶ Marathon

❷ Sanctuary of Artemis at Vravrona

❸ Sanctuary of Eleusis

❹ Daphni Monastery

❺ Monastery of Kaisariani

❻ Temple of Poseidon at Sounion

❻ **Sounion**

Cruise Ship
Terminal

| 0 | 50 mi |
| 0 | 50 km |

Monasteries, temples, and other age-old landmarks surround **Athens** in the hilly landscapes of Attica. Never too far from the sea, these lands are rich in myth and Greek history. The following sights will reveal yet more layers of the labyrinthine history of Greece.

1 Marathon. The race name we use so widely today harks back to 490 B.C. A young man, Pheidippides, ran the 42km (26 miles) from this little town at the edge of the marshy coast to Athens, burst into the Agora, and cried "We've won," then dropped dead from exhaustion. He was announcing the victory of the Athenians, outnumbered three to one, over the Persian army. The Athenians, it seemed, had been miraculously spared. It was said that the mythical hero Theseus appeared to fight alongside the Athenians, and that the god Pan put in an appearance, too. All told, the Persians lost 6,400 warriors and the Athenians just 192. Perhaps humiliated by the defeat, the powerful Persian navy returned to Asia Minor rather than attacking Athens. The Athenian heroes were buried in a mound, the Marathon Tomb, that still rises from the battlefield. There's not much else to see at Marathon, though the site of the Athenians' greatest victory is hallowed ground in Greece. A visit might stir the sort of patriotism that inspired the poet Lord Byron to take up the fight for Greek independence. A fragment of the column that the Athenians erected to celebrate independence is in the Archaeological Museum, about 1.6km (1 mile) from the tomb. *Marathonas.* ☎ *0294/55-155. Admission 3€ for battlefield and museum. Tues–Sun 8:30am–5pm (shorter hours in winter).Buses leave Athens from the station in front of Pedion tou Areos Park every half-hour to hour; the trip costs 5€ and takes 2 hr.*

2 Sanctuary of Artemis at Vravrona. You'll encounter many sanctuaries in Greece where ancient cults worshipped specific deities. This one is especially quirky and charming, terms not always associated with such practices. As legend has it, a young man killed a bear that had attacked his sister, and an epidemic soon broke out. A ceremony in which young girls wore

Marathon.

bear masks and danced was mounted, and the epidemic subsided. So, the bear-dance became a regular event, and a temple to Artemis, goddess of wild animals and the hunt, was built. In yet another twist that always appears in these legends, Iphigenia, the daughter of King Agamemnon who offered herself for sacrifice during the Trojan War to save the women of Greece, became a priestess at the temple. All that remains of the temple to Artemis are some foundations, and a cave is said to be the Tomb of Iphigenia. A restored stoa is lined with bedrooms, complete with small beds and tables, where the young celebrants were housed. Masks, marble heads of the girls, and other artifacts are in the small museum. *Vravrona, 38km (22 miles) east of Athens.* ☎ *22920/27-020. 4€. Tues–Sun 8:30am–5pm (shorter hours in winter). Bus 304 from Athens, Zappion stop; the trip takes about an hour and costs 4€.*

③ Sanctuary of Eleusis. It is hard to imagine that present-day Eleusis, a forest of belching refineries and warehouses 23km (14 miles) west of Athens, was once carpeted with fields and was the realm of Demeter, goddess of the Harvest.

The Sanctuary of Artemis.

The Daphni Monastery.

As the story goes, Hades, god of the underworld, kidnapped Demeter's daughter, Persephone. Demeter came to Eleusis in search of her daughter, and, with the intervention of Zeus (Persephone's father) struck a deal with Hades that Persephone could return to earth for half the year. In gratitude, Demeter equipped Triptolemos, son of the king of Eleusis, with seeds and a chariot in which he could fly around the earth to disperse them. This story inspired the Eleusian Mysteries, rites that celebrated the cycle of life and death. Celebrants from Athens made their way here annually along the Sacred Way, which began in Kerameikos Cemetery (p 59). At Eleusis they engaged in rituals that only the initiated could witness, under pain of death. You can follow the Sacred Way into the Temple of Demeter, where a row of seats surrounds the hall where the rites took place. Much of what remains at the site is Roman—including an arch commemorating Hadrian that inspired the Arc de Triomphe in Paris. *Off I. Agathou, Elefsina.* ☎ *210/554-6019. 4€. Sun–Tues 8:30am–5pm (shorter hours in winter). Bus A16, 853, or 862 from Leoforos Pieros in Omonia; the trip costs 3€ and takes about an hour.*

4 ★★★ **Daphni Monastery.** A trip to this outlying monastery reveals a bit of a surprise: A monastery founded on the site of a temple to Apollo in the 6th century is carpeted in beautiful marble mosaics set in gold. See p 51.

5 **Monastery of Kaisariani.** One of the most tranquil spots close to Athens is this simple monastery at the foot of Mount Hymettus, once carpeted with pine groves that have been decimated in recent fires. The 11th-century complex has ancient roots—it was built on the foundations of a Christian church that in turn replaced a temple to Aphrodite. The surroundings are still surprisingly bucolic, given the proximity of Athens. A spring that rises on the grounds fed the River Illisos, which once flowed near the Acropolis and in antiquity supplied the capital with water. The mountainside was famous for the honey gathered from great swarms of bees. Philosophers brought their students to Kaisariani to escape the heat of the city, as many Athenians still do. Among them are brides who drink from the spring water that still gurgles forth near the entrance to the monastery and is said to help

induce pregnancy. *Off Academias St. Kaisariani (about 10km/6 miles from center of Athens).* ☎ *210/723-6619. Admission 4€. Tues–Sun 8:30am–5pm (shorter hours in summer). Bus 224 from Plateia Kaningos, near Syntagma. The trip takes about half an hour; you will need to walk about 2km (1 mile) from the center of Kaisarani to the monastery.*

6 ★★★ **Temple of Poseidon at Sounion.** Fifteen of the original 34 columns still surround this temple to the god of the sea commanding a 29m (95-ft.) bluff at the southernmost tip of Attica. The rugged coast below the temple has changed little since ancient times, making it easy to imagine the joy the landmark elicited in sailors, a sign they were nearing home. Or, for that matter, looking over the sea from the temple, you can understand its role as a lookout post from which sentinels kept watch for approaching warships during the Peloponnesian Wars. Many visitors come to watch the sunset from the temple; if you wish to join them, you can kill time by looking for the place on one of the columns where Lord Byron carved his name. See p 20.

The Temple of Poseidon at Sounion.

South Coast Beaches

- **1** Asteria Glyfada
- **2** Voula A
- **3** Thalassea
- **4** Vouliagmeni
- **5** Yabanaki Varkiza

It doesn't take much to get an Athenian to the beach—and when summertime temperatures hit 46°C (115°F) in the shade, you'll see the appeal. Fortunately, it's easy to get to a beach near Athens. A nice string of sand follows the coastline south of the city, known as the Apollo Coast. You'll pay to get onto these beaches, where you can rent sunbeds, umbrellas, and all sorts of other amenities. START: **Metro to Syntagma.**

1 kids **Asteria Glyfada.** Notice the Miami Beach vibe: white recliners, white umbrellas, even white sand (imported). A string of bars will deliver drinks to your lounge chair. The water can be a bit shallow and murky, but most patrons are too caught up in the scene to care. *58 Poseidonos Ave. (17km/11 miles south of Athens).* ☎ *210/894-4548. www.balux-septem.com. Daily 8:30am–9pm, beach bars 9am–1am. Admission 7€ Mon–Fri, 11€*

Sat–Sun/holidays, children half-price. Tram: Metaxa St. or bus: A1, A2, E1, E2, E22.

2 kids **Voula A.** The regular crowds of 20-somethings and teenagers don't seem to mind that the beach is pebbly in spots and, unless you snag a sun bed, there's no shade. You'll find a lot more than sand and surf here: a swimming pool, a snack bar, water slides and watersports gear (skis, tubes, and boards), parachuting, pedal boats,

Suburban Glyfada has a Miami vibe, with a sandy beach backed by bars and lounges.

racquetball, beach volleyball, minisoccer, some bars, and a mini-market. *4 Alkyonidon St. (19km/12 miles south of Athens).* ☎ *210/895-9632. www.apollonies.gr. Daily 8am–sunset (beach closes); beachfront cafe & other facilities stay open at night. Admission 4€ adults, 1.50€ children 6–12 & seniors. Tram: Asklipiou Voulas St. or bus: A2, E1, E2, E22, 114, 116, 149, 340.*

❸ kids Thalassea. Also known as Voula B, this stretch of sand is a bit less of a scene than its neighbor, and the waters are calm and clean, protected by break waters. *20km (12 miles) southeast of Athens.* ☎ *210/895-9632. www.thalassea. gr. Daily 8am–sunset. Admission Mon–Fri 5€; Sat–Sun & holidays 6€; includes sun beds, umbrellas. Bus: A2, E1, E2, E22, 114, 116, 149, 340.*

❹ kids Vouliagmeni. One of Athens's favorite beach getaways has a bit of everything: trees, shade, and sand and sea so sparkling that the beach has earned the European blue flag for cleanliness. There's even a ruined temple down the road, and if you desire a curative soak, Lake Vouliagmeni, just south of town, maintains a constant 24°C (75°F) temperature year-round. *Poseidonos Ave. (25km/16 miles south of Athens).* ☎ *210/967-3184. Admission 4€; 60 & over, 6–12 years 1.50€. Bus: E22 or from Glyfada: 114, 116, 149.*

❺ Yabanaki Varkiza. With rows of sun beds and blaring beach bars, this very popular beach is hardly a quiet getaway. But the drive here winds along the spectacular cliffs of the Attica peninsula and just beyond; along the route to Cape Sounion, the rocky coastline is etched with coves that are great for snorkeling and swimming. *Sounion Ave. (30km/19 miles southeast of Athens).* ☎ *210/897-2414. www. yabanaki.gr. May 1–Sept 30 daily 8am–8pm. Admission 5.50€ Mon–Fri; 7€ Sat–Sun; 3.50€ children 6–12, students & seniors; 5 & under free. Sat–Sun 4€ sun beds/umbrellas. Bus: E22, 170, 171, or 340.*

The rocky coves past Varkiza along the route to Cape Sounion offer opportunities for swimming and snorkeling but are unguarded.

Nearby **Island Escapes**

W hen the heat in Athens gets to be too much, do as the Athenians do—get on a boat and head to a nearby island in the Saronic Gulf. Aegina, Poros, and Hydra lace the waters south of Athens off the coast of the Peloponnesian Peninsula. To reach any of them, all you need to do is take the Metro to Piraeus and board a hydrofoil; the farthest of the three main islands, Hydra, is only 90 minutes away. START: **Metro to Pireaus.**

1 **Aegina.** The largest island in the Saronic Gulf is so close to Athens that many islanders commute to the capital for work. Take a walk along the waterfront of Aegina Town, where a morning fish market operates, and follow winding stone streets to the **Markelos Tower,** a Venetian-era fortified house that in 1827 hosted meetings of the first government in Greece. The ruins of the island's longtime capital, **Palechora,** sprawl across a hillside 5km (3 miles) south of Aegina Town; a number of Byzantine churches are still in use, and many are decorated with faded frescoes. The beautifully preserved **Temple of Aphaia** (12km/7 miles east of Aegina Town;

Clear, shallow, inviting waters wash against the sandy headlands around Skala on Angistri.

☎ 22970/32-398; www.culture greece.com; admission 4€; Apr–Nov daily 8:30am–7pm, Dec–Mar daily 8:15am–3pm; hourly bus from Aegina Town) commands a promontory facing Athens and the coast of Attica. Both the Parthenon and Temple of Poseidon can be seen on a clear day (with the aid of binoculars). While 25 columns remain standing, what's not here is a magnificent pediment frieze depicting scenes from the Trojan War, now in the Glyptothek in Munich. Nearby **Angistri,** a short ferry ride away, is ringed with clean, sandy beaches.

2 **Poros.** Barely an island at all, Poros is separated from the mainland by a channel only 370m (1,214 ft.) wide—Poros means "straits." Car ferries bring many cars and many visitors to Poros in the summer, but you may wish to do the reverse and head over to the mainland after taking a quick look around. The scant remains of the **Temple of Poseidon** (5km/3 miles south of Poros Town) might evoke the memory of Demonsthenes, the great 4th-century B.C. Athenian orator who took refuge here when Macedonians attacked Athens. When discovered, he asked to write one last letter and bit the nib off his pen to release concealed poison. The orator's remains allegedly lie beneath a monument **Monastery of Zoodochos Pigi** (Source of Life), where a spring is believed to have curative powers. You can fill a bottle or two at the spring (3km/2 miles from Poros Town; ☎ 22980/22-926;

The Great Outdoors

Getting to the Islands

For schedules, check the websites www.ferries.gr or www.gtp.gr; you can also get schedules from offices of the **Greek National Tourism Organization** (www.gnto.gr). **Hellenic Seaways** (☎ 210/419-9200, www.hellenicseaways.gr) is one of several companies that provide speedy hydrofoil service to Aegina (40 min., about 15€), Poros (1 hr., about 17€), and Hydra (90 min., about 22€); departures are roughly every hour to 2 hours during high season.

May–Sept daily 8am–1:30pm and 4:30–8:30pm, Oct–Apr daily 8am–1:30pm and 4:30–5:30pm) to determine if this is true. For the best beach experience on Poros, cross back to the mainland, where the Galatas region is part of the island's holdings. A 5-minute ferry ride to Galatas and a 10-minute taxi ride brings you to **Aliki**, a lovely stretch of sand on a spit wedged between the bay and a lake. In the spring and early summer, the shoreline is scented with lemons that are grown in surrounding groves.

③ **Hydra.** Seafaring families built beautiful stone mansions on Hydra in the late 18th and early 19th centuries, artists and writers began arriving in the 1960s, and in their wake came the rich and famous and the simply rich. They keep a low profile, and with the absence of cars (transport is by foot or mule), Hydra seems wonderfully removed from the modern world. Hikers can set off through the herb-scented countryside for several remote religious outposts about an hour from the port: the **Convent of Ayia Efpraxia, Monastery of the Prophet Elijah,** and the **Monastery of Ayios Nikolaos.** The views from all are spectacular. Swimming from the rocks of the rugged shoreline is an exhilarating way to enjoy the warm Aegean waters, and a pleasant waterside walk west from Hydra Town brings you to especially nice spots at **Spilla** and **Kamini.** ●

An alley in the fishing village of Poros.

Dining **Best Bets**

Best **Exotic Food**
★ Altamira $$$ *36A Tsakalof St.* *(p 102)*

Best **Place to Dine Like an Ancient Greek**
★ Archaion Gefsis $$ *22 Kodratou St.* *(p 102)*

Best **Museum Fare**
★ Benaki Museum Cafe $$ *1 Koumbari St.* *(p 103)*

Best **French Bistro**
★ Chez Lucien $$ *32 Troon St.* *(p 103)*

Best **Place for Romance**
★★★ GB Roof Garden $$$$ *Grande Bretagne Hotel, Syntagma Sq.* *(p 105)*

Best **Place for Romance Without Breaking the Bank**
★ Filistron $$ *24 Apostolou Pavlou St.* *(p 104)*

Best **Trendy Taverna**
★ Mamacas $$ *41 Persephonis St.* *(p 105)*

Best **Place to Soak in a View of the City**
★ Orizontes $$$$$ *Aristippou & Ploutarchou sts.* *(p 106)*

Best **Place to Rub Shoulders with Locals**
★★ Papandreou's $ *Meat Market, Agora* *(p 106)*

Best **Meze**
★★ Rozalia $ *58 Valtetsiou St.* *(p 107)*

Best **Place to Eat with a Group**
★ Kouklis (Scholarhio) Ouzeri $ *14 Tripodon St.* *(p 105)*

Best **Grill**
★★★ Telis $ *86 Evripidou St.* *(p 107)*

Best **Seafood**
★★ Thalatta $$ *5 Vitonos St.* *(p 108)*

Best **Old World Cafe**
★★ Café Avissinia $ *7 Kinetou St.* *(p 103)*

This page: People dining in gentrified Psyrri, which is overflowing with bars, ouzeries, and cafes.
Previous page: The Acropolis, as seen from the rooftop restaurant of the King George Palace hotel.

Lycabettus Dining

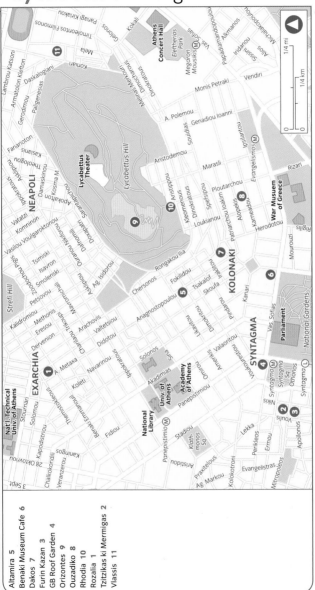

Altamira 5
Benaki Museum Cafe 6
Dakos 7
Furin Kazan 3
GB Roof Garden 4
Orizontes 9
Ouzadiko 8
Rhodia 10
Rozalia 1
Tzitzikas ki Mermigas 2
Vlassis 11

Psyrri & Plaka Dining

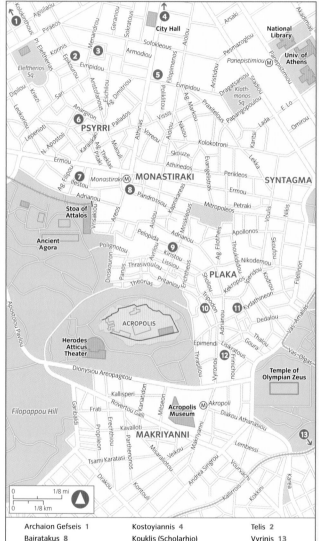

Archaion Gefseis 1
Bairatakus 8
Bar Guru Bar 3
Café Avissinia 7
Daphne's 12

Kostoyiannis 4
Kouklis (Scholarhio)
 Ouzeri 10
Papandreou's 5
Platanos Taverna 9

Telis 2
Vyrinis 13
Vyzantino 11
Zeidoron 6

Gazi, Thissio & Koukaki Dining

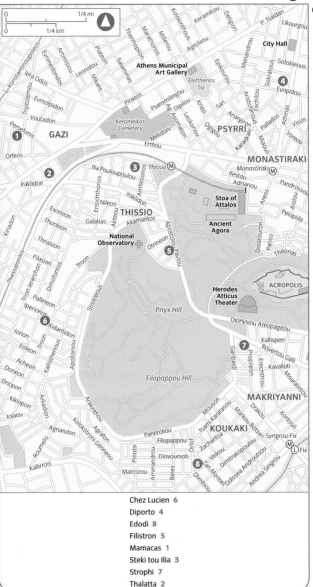

Chez Lucien 6

Diporto 4

Edodi 8

Filistron 5

Mamacas 1

Steki tou Ilia 3

Strophi 7

Thalatta 2

Athens Dining A to Z

Altamira serves cuisines from around the world.

★ **Altamira** KOLONAKI *FUSION*
Fusion cuisine hits a new extreme in these elegant surroundings where dishes are infused with Middle Eastern, Indian, and Southeast Asian flavors. For an even more exotic experience, order one of the daily special preparations of reindeer, ostrich, or other wild game. *36A Tsakalof St.* ☎ *210/361-4695 or 210/363-9906. Entrees 15€–25€. MC, V. Mon–Sat 1pm–1:30am; closed mid-July to Aug. Metro: Syntagma or bus: 200. Map p 99.*

The chef at Archaion Gefsis has used archaeological records to prepare foods eaten in ancient Greece.

★ **Archaion Gefsis** METAXOURGIO *TRADITIONAL GREEK* Lying on a couch being served by toga clad waiters may seem a bit gimmicky (or just plain decadent), but even Athenians enjoy stepping back in time here to dip into fare based on ancient recipes. *22 Kodratou St.* ☎ *210/523-9661. Entrees 20€–25€. AE, DC, MC, V. Tues–Sat 7pm–1am; Sun noon–5pm; closed 2 weeks in Aug. Reservations essential. Map p 100.*

Bairaktaris MONASTIRAKI *GREEK*
This century-old fixture in Monastiraki Square never seems to change, and that's how the loyal following likes it. A *magirefta* (one-pot meal cooked on the stove) is always on offer, along with meze, kebabs, and other straightforward taverna standards. *2 Monastiraki Sq.* ☎ *210/321-3036. Entrees 5€–10€. AE, MC, V. Daily 10am–1am. Metro: Monastiraki. Map p 100.*

Bar Guru Bar AGORA *THAI*
Excellent Thai food is accompanied by a nice selection of cocktails and, on many evenings, mellow jazz. *10 Theatrou Sq.* ☎ *210/324-6530. Entrees 15€. AE, DC, MC, V. Mon–Thurs 9:30pm–1am; Fri–Sat*

9:30pm–1:30am. Metro: Omonia or Monastiraki. Map p 100.

★ **Benaki Museum Cafe** KOLONAKI *CONTINENTAL* Museums don't often rank as great places to dine, but don't think of visiting this wonderful collection without enjoying a meal in the bright and airy rooftop cafe. Lunches, including Greek staples as well as quiches and other light fare, are excellent, and the Thursday-night buffet is especially popular, even with locals—reservations are recommended. *1 Koumbari St. at Vas. Sofias Ave.* ☎ *210/367-1000. www.benaki.gr. Entrees 12€. AE, DC, MC, V. Mon, Wed & Fri–Sat 9am–5pm; Thurs 9am–midnight; Sun 9am–3pm; closed Tues, holidays. Metro: Syntagma. Map p 99.*

★★ **Café Avissinia** MONASTIRAKI *TAVERNA* Take refuge from the surrounding flea market in these mahogany-paneled rooms, where homey seafood dishes and other traditional fare is washed down with the delicious house wine. *7 Kinetou St. at Abyssinia Sq.* ☎ *210/321-7047. www.avissinia.gr. Entrees 10€–15€. MC, V. Tues–Sat 11:30am–1am; Sun 11am–7pm; closed mid-July to Aug. Metro: Monastiraki. Map p 100.*

★ **Chez Lucien** ANO PETRALONA *FRENCH* You will probably have to wait for one of the shared tables, but the French-bistro fare is delicious and much less expensive than what's on offer at some of the capital's other outposts of French cooking. *32 Troon St.* ☎ *210/346-4236. Entrees 18€–25€. No credit cards. Daily 8:30pm–2am; closed Christmas week, 2 weeks at Easter, Aug. Reservations not accepted. Metro: Thissio or bus 227. Map p 101.*

★★ **Dakos** KOLONAKI *CRETAN* The island of Crete is deservedly renowned for its simple cuisine based on wholesome ingredients, and this handsome white room delights diners with island specialties. The namesake Dakos (a salad of feta, tomatoes, and rusks) deservedly gets a prominent place on the menu, along with pies stuffed with cheese and vegetables, mountain greens, country sausage, and many other delicious Cretan staples. *6 Tsakalof St.* ☎ *210/360-4020. Entrees 12€–25€. MC, V. Daily 7–11pm. Metro: Syntagma. Map p 99.*

★★ **Daphne's** PLAKA *GREEK* A 1830s mansion with frescoed rooms and a leafy courtyard provides one of the city's most romantic dining experiences. Rabbit stewed in wine and other delicious takes on traditional fare do justice to the surroundings. *4 Lysikratous St.* ☎ *210/322-7971. Entrees 15€–30€. AE, DC, MC, V.*

Café Avissinia serves Greek favorites amid old world surroundings.

Restaurant Fast Facts

Eating out is a national pastime in Athens, and fresh ingredients are the staples of Greek cooking. Most restaurants, except those in hotels and those that cater to tourists, are usually closed on either Sunday, Monday, or Tuesday, as well as on Christmas, New Year's Day, Easter, and on and around August 15 (the Assumption of the Virgin Mary). Unless stated otherwise, the closing times listed are when the kitchen closes, not the restaurant—it is a rare proprietor who would kick out a patron. As for tipping, restaurants may include a service charge, but an extra 10% to 15% for the waiter or busboy is appreciated.

Daily 7pm–1am. Metro: Syntagma. Map p 100.

Diporto OMONIA *GREEK* Not a whiff of pretense pervades this simple lunch room in the central market where delicious stews, platters of *gigantes* (butter beans), and other hearty dishes are served to vendors from the surrounding stalls. *Central Market, Athinas St. Entrees 4€–8€. AE, DC, MC, V. Mon–Sat 6am–6pm. Metro: Monastiraki. Map p 101.*

Filistron, as seen from Apostolou Pavlou Street, serves classic Greek dishes, as well as unusual regional Greek food.

★★ **Edodi** KOUKAKI *MODERN GREEK* An old mansion is the setting for some of the city's finest fare, with a menu that changes daily according to what's freshest in the market—ingredients are brought to your table and then prepared to your liking. Such attention to detail comes at a price, but you'll not soon forget your meal here. **Warning:** The restaurant is at the top of a steep staircase. *80 Veikou St.* ☎ *210/921-3013. Entrees 35€–40€. AE, DC, MC, V. Mon–Sat 8pm–12:30am; closed July–Aug. Reservations recommended. Metro: Syngrou-Fix or trolley: 1, 5, 15. Map p 101.*

★ **Filistron** THISSIO *REGIONAL GREEK* A meal-in-themselves selection of meze come with a million-dollar view of the Acropolis—for a nice meal at a good price, it's hard to do much better in Athens. *24 Apostolou Pavlou St.* ☎ *210/346-7554. Entrees 12€. DC, MC, V. Oct–May Tues–Sun noon–1am; June–Sept Tues–Sun 6pm–1am. Metro: Thissio. Reservations recommended. Map p 101.*

★ **Furin Kazan** SYNTAGMA *JAPANESE* It only stands to reason that fish, such a player in Greek cuisine, could also make an appearance in sushi and sashimi—most successfully, as the crowds of Japanese businessmen and Athenians attest. *2 Apollonos St.* ☎ *210/322-9170. Entrees 10€–20€. AE, DC, MC, V. Mon–Sat noon–11:30pm; Sun 2–11:30pm. Metro: Syntagma. Map p 99.*

★★★ **GB Roof Garden** SYN-TAGMA *MEDITERRANEAN* Politicians, royalty, and Hollywood stars have all raved about their meals—accompanied by knockout Acropolis views—atop the city's swankiest hotel. You can join them for breakfast, lunch, or dinner or just come for a cocktail at sunset. *Grande Bretagne Hotel, Syntagma Sq.* ☎ *210/333-0000. www.grandebretagne.gr. Entrees 30€–50€. AE, DC, MC, V. Daily 6:30–11am & 1pm–1:15am; New Year's Eve 8pm–3:30am; New Year's Day 1–4pm; reduced holiday hours. Metro: Syntagma. Map p 99.*

Kostoyiannis OMONIA *GREEK* A fixture in the commercial heart of Athens for more than 50 years is handsomely traditional and serves food in the same vein—hearty *stifados* (meat stews), chops, and plain preparations of superbly fresh seafood are served in the old-fashioned dining room. *37 Zaimi St.* ☎ *210/822-0624. Entrees 15€–25€. No credit cards. Mon–Sat 8pm–midnight. Metro: Omonia. Map p 100.*

★ **Kouklis (Scholarhio) Ouzeri** PLAKA *MEZE/TAVERNA* Bring a

Scholarhio, as it's commonly known, serves meze dishes, such as fried eggplant or marinated peppers.

group and choose from a tray of delicious appetizers—tzatziki, moussaka, taramosalata, fried eggplant, and dozens of others. A selection of dishes, wine, mineral water, and dessert go for 14€ per person—the more people at the table, the more dishes you get to try. *14 Tripodon St.* ☎ *210/324-7605. www. sholarhio.gr. Meze 2.50€–5€. MC, V. Daily 11am–2am. Metro: Syntagma or Monastiraki. Map p 100.*

★ **Mamacas** GAZI *MODERN GREEK* One of the first of the city's "neo

Fast Food a la Greque

As much as Athenians enjoy a leisurely meal, like city folk everywhere they must sometimes eat on the run. Sidewalk stands serving souvlaki and gyros are ubiquitous, and a few chains also serve those on the go. **Everest** specializes in what Europeans call "toasts": flat sandwich buns filled with meat and cheese and grilled (about 4€); an especially popular outlet is the one on Kolonaki Square. **Neon** is the city's most popular cafeteria, serving up hearty portions of pasta, salads, and sandwiches (main courses 5€–10€) in outlets in Syntagma and Omonia Squares and other city hubs.

tavernas" helped plant formerly industrial Gazi on the nightlife map. The decor is white-washed and mini-malist, but the kitchen sends out the sorts of meals that Greek moms serve (the name means "mommy"). 41 Persephonis St. ☎ 210/346-4984. www.mamacas.gr. Entrees 20€–30€. Daily 1:30pm–1:30am. AE, MC, V. Metro: Kerameikos. Map p 101.

★ **Orizontes** KOLONAKI *CONTI-NENTAL/SEAFOOD* The Acropolis, the modern city, and the Aegean are spread out at your feet from this perch high atop Mt. Lycabettus. You can sample several seafood dishes on a tasting menu (the restaurant is operated by a large seafood whole-saler) or select from a menu that also includes several meat dishes. The adjoining **Cafe Lycabettus** is much less formal and less expensive but shares the million-dollar views. Aristippou & Ploutarchou sts. ☎ 210/721-0701. www.kastelorizo. com.gr. Entrees 30€–40€; cafe entrees 15€. AE, MC, V. Daily 9am–2am. Bus: 022, 060, 200 to the funic-ular. Map p 99.

Ouzadiko KOLONAKI *MEZE* A lively *ouzeri* in the atrium of the Lemos shopping center is wildly popular with business folks, who put together meals from a choice of dozens of meze (the meatballs, fried anchovies, and mountain greens are standouts) and 40 types of ouzo. *Lemos International Centre, 25–29 Karneadou St.* ☎ *210/729-5484. Entrees 16€–25€; meze from 3€. AE, DC, MC, V. Mon–Sat 12:30pm–midnight; closed Christmas, New Year's Day, Easter & Aug. Metro: Evangelismos. Map p 99.*

★★ **Papandreou's** AGORA *TAV-ERNA* Late-night clubbers and surly loners rub elbows at one of the city's favorite after-hours stops. Big portions of soup (tripe is espe-cially popular), stews, and square meals are served round-the-clock near one of the entrances to the Central Market. *1 Aristogeitonos St. at Evripidou St. (inside the Agora meat market).* ☎ *213/008-2242. Entrees 6€–10€. V. Daily 24 hr. Metro: Omonia, Panepistimiou, or Monastiraki. Map p 100.*

Platanos Taverna PLAKA *TAV-ERNA* A beloved institution, estab-lished in 1932, is a standout amid its tourist-trap neighbors; the succulent roast lamb brings regulars back time after time and can be enjoyed in a pretty courtyard. *4 Dioyenous St.* ☎ *210/322-0666. Entrees 10€–11€. No credit cards. Mon–Sat noon–4:30pm & 7:30pm–midnight; closed*

The view from Orizontes, perched atop Mt. Lycabettus.

The spanakorizo (spinach risotto) at Rozalia makes a good meze starter.

Sun, 2 weeks in Aug. Metro: Monastiraki or Syntagma. Map p 100.

★ **Rhodia** KOLONAKI *TAVERNA* Even the well-heeled residents of fashionable Kolonaki enjoy a good taverna meal, and this handsome old house with a garden is a local institution in the neighborhood. Hearty favorites include dolmades in lemon sauce, some of the best to be had in Athens. *44 Aristipou St.* ☎ *210/722-9883. Entrees 10€–20€. No credit cards. Mon–Sat 8pm–2am. Metro: Syntagma. Map p 99.*

★★ **Rozalia** EXARCHIA *MEZE/TAVERNA* Popular with generations of students at the nearby university, this family-run operation serves 15 kinds of meze—and in the unlikely event you still have an appetite, they can be followed up with grilled meat and fish. A fan-cooled garden is a welcome warm-weather retreat in the busy neighborhood. *58 Valtetsiou St.* ☎ *210/330-2933. Entrees 6€–8€. DC, MC, V. Daily 11am–2am; closed Jan 1, Dec 25. Metro: Omonia. Map p 99.*

★★ **Steki tou Ilia** THISSIO *TAVERNA* A grillhouse that operates on two sides of a pedestrian street serves what might be the best lamb chops in town, accompanied by

grilled bread topped with herbs. *5 Eptahalkou St.* ☎ *210/345-8052; 7 Thessalonikis St.* ☎ *210/342-2407. Entrees 8€–18€. No credit cards. Mon–Sat 1pm–1am; Sun 1–5:30pm. Eptahalkou closed last 2 weeks in Aug; Thessalonikis closed first 2 weeks in Aug. Metro: Thissio. Map p 101.*

Strophi ACROPOLIS *TAVERNA* As comfortable as a well-worn shoe, this classic taverna near the Odeon of Herodes Atticus serves a traditional menu of meze and oven roasted meats. Predictable as the offerings are, the place still manages to wow with views of the Acropolis from the rooftop garden. *25 Rovertou Galli St.* ☎ *210/921-4130. Entrees 12€–20€. MC, V. Mon–Sat 7pm–1am; closed Sun, Jan 1, Easter & Dec 25. Bus: 230. Map p 101.*

★★★ **Telis** PSYRRI *GRILL* What this haven for carnivores might lack in atmosphere it makes up for with quantity. Stacks of grilled pork and lamb chops seem to appear on the table the moment you sit down. *86 Evripidou St. at Koumoundourou Sq.* ☎ *210/324-2775. Entrees 7€–10€. No credit cards. Mon–Sat 11am–2am; closed Sun, part of Aug. Bus: 100, 200. Map p 100.*

Tables at Steki tou Ilia spill onto the street.

★★ **Thalatta** THISSIO/GAZI *SEA-FOOD* Former seafarer turned restaurateur Yannis Safos is obsessed with freshness. The seafood he serves, including the city's best selection of shellfish, seems to jump from the Aegean right onto your table in the pretty courtyard or in the elegant dining room. *5 Vitonos & 105 Piraeos sts., Gefyra Poulopoulou.* ☎ *210/346-4204. Entrees 20€– 40€. AE, DC, MC, V. Nov–Apr Mon–Sat 8pm–1:30am; Sun noon– 6pm. Metro: Kerameikos or Thissio or bus/trolley: B18, G18, 21, 035, 049, 227, 400. Map p 101.*

★ **Tzitzikas kai Mermigas** SYNTAGMA *MODERN GREEK* Kebabs, meat and vegetable pies, onions stuffed with bacon, and other traditional fare is served on tables topped with butcher paper in a whimsically retro room that evokes an old-fashioned grocery store. The food and decor is a big hit with Athenians: You'll find several other branches around town. *12–14 Mitropoleos St.* ☎ *210/324-7607. Meze 4€–8€. MC, V. Mon–Sat 1pm– 1am; closed holidays, 2 weeks in Aug. Metro: Syntagma. Map p 99.*

Tzitzikas kai Mermigas, which is reminiscent of a country kitchen or general store.

★★ **Vlassis** AMPELOKIPI *GREEK* For a home-cooked meal, do what the Athenians do and head to this neoclassical mansion in a quiet neighborhood near the American Embassy. Dozens of salads, spreads, and small meat and seafood dishes are brought to the table and you pick what you want—be forewarned that you will be tempted to take more than you can eat. *8 Paster St.* ☎ *210/646-3060. Dishes 5€–15€. AE, DC, MC, V. Daily 11am–1am. Metro: Syntagma. Map p 99.*

★ **Vyrinis** ACROPOLIS *GREEK* A summertime meal at this popular neighborhood spot is like a country outing. The large garden is surrounded by the green acreage around the Panathenaic Stadium, and pork and lamb sizzle on the grill. Wintertime meals in a room lined with wine casks are a pleasure, too. *8 Archimidou St.* ☎ *210/701-2153. Entrees 7€–15€. MC, V. Mon–Sat noon–11am, Sun noon–5pm. Metro: Acropolis. Map p 100.*

★ **Vyzantino** PLAKA *TAVERNA* You can't go wrong at this Plaka mainstay, where a steady stream of passers-by is the backdrop for a meal of moussaka and other taverna staples on the sidewalk terrace. Neighborhood regulars turn up in droves for lunch. *18 Kydathineon St.* ☎ *210/322-7368. Entrees 10€–15€. AE, DC, MC, V. Daily 7am–1am. Metro: Syntagma. Map p 100.*

Zeidoron PSYRRI *MEZE* Tables along the pedestrian street out front provide a bird's-eye view of comings and goings in Athens's trendiest nighttime neighborhood. The selection of wine and meze is huge, and heartier fare is also available. *10 Taki St. at Agia Anargyron St.* ☎ *210/321-5368. Entrees 11€–15€; meze 3€–5€. AE, MC, V. Mon–Thurs 6pm–2am; Fri–Sun noon–2am; closed 1 week in Aug. Metro: Monastiraki. Map p 100. ●*

Nightlife Best Bets

Best Glamorous Seaside Lounge
★★ Akrotiri Lounge, *B5 Vas. Georgiou St. (p 114)*

Best Hotel Bar
★★ Alexander's Bar, *Hotel Grande Bretagne, Syntagma Sq. (p 115)*

Best Bar with a Panoramic View
★ Galaxy Bar, *Hilton Hotel, 46 Vas. Sofias Ave. (p 117)*

Best Cafe-Bar for Model-Watching
★ Jackson Hall, *4 Milioni St. (p 114)*

Best Rooftop Lounge
★★ Air Lounge, *Fresh Hotel, 26 Sofokleous St. at Kleisthenous St. (p 115)*

Best Trendy Scene
★ Mamacas, *41 Persefonis St. (p 117)*

Best (and Only) Irish Bar
Mike's Irish Bar, *6 Sinopis St. (p 117)*

Best Place to Be on the Cutting Edge of Clubdom
★ Nipiagogio, *8 Kleanthous St. (p 117)*

Best Place to Rub Shoulders with Spoiled Athenian Youth
★ Envy, *Monastiraki Center, 3 Agias Eleousis St. (p 118)*

Best Cafe-Bar for Alt Rock
★ Stavlos, *10 Iraklidon St. (p 115)*

Best for Romance
★★★ Thirio, *1 Lepeniotou St. (p 118)*

Best Outdoor Lounge
★ Baraonda, *Tsoha 23. (p 115)*

Best for Dancing
★ Six D.O.G.S. *Avrarmiotou 6–8 (p 120)*

This page: The rooftop terrace of Galaxy Bar, in the landmark Hilton Athens, is popular with celebrities and guests of the hotel.
Previous page: Athens's lively nightlife scene.

Lycabettus Nightlife

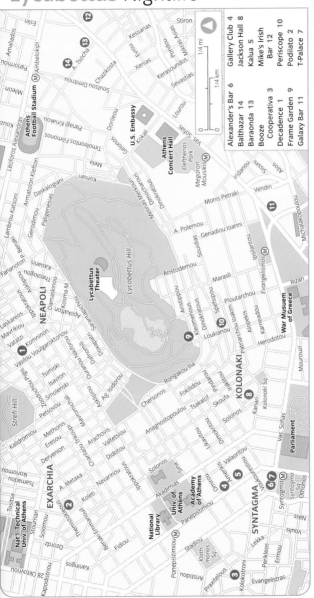

Nightlife Best Bets

Alexander's Bar 6
Balthazar 14
Baranda 13
Booze
  Cooperativa 3
Decadence 1
Frame Garden 9
Galaxy Bar 11
Gallery Club 4
Jackson Hall 8
Kalua 5
Mike's Irish
  Bar 12
Periscope 10
Podilato 2
T-Palace 7

Psyrri & Plaka Nightlife

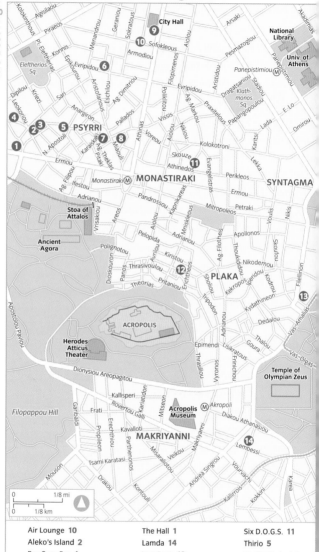

Air Lounge 10
Aleko's Island 2
Bar Guru Bar 6
Cubanita Havana Club 7
Envy 8

The Hall 1
Lamda 14
LavaBore 13
Moet & Chandon 9
Pop 12

Six D.O.G.S. 11
Thirio 5
Vanilla Project 3
Venti 4

Gazi & Thissio Nightlife

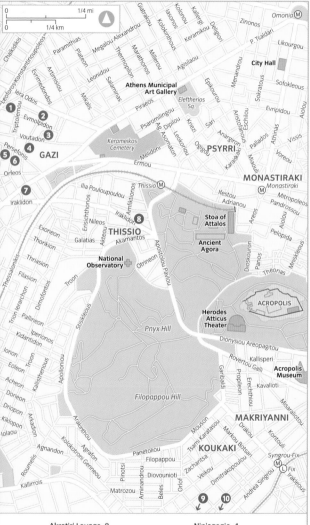

Akrotiri Lounge 9
Bios 7
45 Degrees 3
Mad Club 5
Mamacas 6

Nipiagogio 4
Noiz Club 2
Romeo 10
Sodade 1
Stavlos 8

Athens Nightlife A to Z

Bar- & Club-Restaurants

★★ Akrotiri Lounge AGIOS KOS-MAS   One of Athens's most popular seaside playgrounds is stylish and just plain fun, with tropical decor, a beach, a big swimming pool, many dance floors and bars, very decent Mediterranean cuisine, and excellent music that runs the gamut from Greek to hip-hop and R&B. It's about 6.8km (4¼ miles) from central Athens, along the coast. *B5 Vas. Georgiou St., Kalamaki.* ☎ *210/985-9147. www.akrotirilounge.gr. Nov–Apr Fri–Sat 15€ cover; May–Oct Mon–Thurs 15€ cover, Fri–Sun 20€ cover. Tram: 2nd Agia Kosma or bus: A1, A2. Map p 113.*

Cubanita Havana Club PSYRRI Cuban cuisine, cigars, and excellent mojitos are paired with live Latin music. *28 Karaiskaki St. at Psyrri Sq.* ☎ *210/331-4605. www.cubanita.gr. Closed Aug. 15€ cover w/drink. Metro: Monastiraki. Map p 112.*

★ Jackson Hall KOLONAKI   One of the best known night spots in fashionable Kolonaki is an American-style

The Cubanita Havana Club is small but lively, and the best place for Latin dancing in the city.

diner decorated with Hollywood memorabilia that serves the best burgers and fries in town. The crowd, however, is fashionably European, including the models who are making ends meet by waitressing (and what

Athens by Night

Cafes, bars, and clubs are almost as common as eating establishments in Athens—which probably means that Athenians like to party, drink, and dance as much as they like to eat. Venues come and go all the time, and many of the bigger dance clubs close up shop in Athens for the summer and move out to the sea coast. To keep up with the latest clubs and to find out who's performing when and where, check out the English language **Athens News** (www.athensnews.gr), hotel handouts such as **Welcome to Athens** and **Best of Athens,** and www.athensnights.gr and other websites. Most nightspots don't heat up until midnight, and many don't even open until 11pm or later and stay open until 5 or 6am— all the more amazing considering that many of the habitués have to report for work in the morning.

could be more American than that?) and their more successful counterparts who populate the bar. *4 Milioni St.* ☎ *210/361-6098. Metro: Syntagma. Map p 111.*

★ **Stavlos** THISSIO The former royal stables now do multiple duty as a bar, restaurant (decent Italian-Mediterranean food), and an easy-going sidewalk cafe where regulars sit for hours and watch the action on pedestrian Iraklidon Street. Art exhibits are often on view, films are sometimes screened, and a DJ turns up most nights to spin alternative rock. *10 Iraklidon St.* ☎ *210/346-7206 or 210/345-2502. Metro: Thissio. Map p 113.*

Bars & Lounges

★★ **Air Lounge** OMONIA Get away from it all atop the trendy Fresh Hotel—an outdoor garden that surrounds the pool and overlooks the Acropolis is hands-down one of the most relaxing spots in the busy and gritty center of town. *Fresh Hotel, 26 Sofokleous St. at Kleisthenous St.* ☎ *210/524-8511. www.freshhotel.gr. Metro: Omonia. Map p 112.*

★★ **Alexander's Bar** SYNTAGMA Alexander the Great, centerpiece of an 18th-century tapestry hanging over the bar, keeps an eye on goings-on at what many seasoned travelers claim is the best hotel lounge in the world. A clubby atmosphere, along with a huge selection of single malt Scotches and cigars (dispensed from a walk-in humidor), give the place a good-old-boy atmosphere, but in these upscale environs the "old boy" next to you may well be a prince or oil baron. Try the house's signature drink, a delicious concoction laced with the oils of Sicilian tangerines. *Hotel Grande Bretagne, Syntagma Sq.* ☎ *210/333-0000. www.grandebretagne.gr. Metro: Syntagma. Map p 111.*

★ **Balthazar** AMBELOKIPI A beautiful courtyard garden and the elegant interiors of a neoclassical mansion attract a well-heeled crowd who enjoy lounge music and a light menu. *Tsoha 27.* ☎ *210/644-1215. www.balthazar.gr. Daily 10pm–late. Metro: Ambelokipi. Map p 111.*

★ **Baraonda** AMBELOKIPI This neighbor of Balthazar may well be the most glamorous outdoors spot in Athens, catering to international business people as well as Athenians out for a polished night on the town. A DJ is often on hand to spin an international mix and the food is much more than an afterthought. *Tsoha 23.* ☎ *210/644-4308. www.baraonda.gr. Daily 10pm–late. Metro: Ambelokipi. Map p 111.*

★ **Bar Guru Bar** AGORA The best of the city's few Thai restaurants does double duty as a lounge that features jazz (sometimes live)

Stavlos is part restaurant, bar, lounge, and even art gallery—it hosts exhibitions and film screenings.

Bouzoukia nights in Athens are best when fueled by an ouzo or two.

that is especially intoxicating beneath the Chinese lanterns swaying in the breeze of a fan. *10 Theatrou Sq.* ☎ *210/324-6530. Metro: Omonia or Monastiraki. Map p 112.*

★ **Bios** GAZI   Athens has a few hybrids like this that do multi-duty as clubs, screening rooms, art galleries, and cafes. Bios adds to the mix with excellent music in a basement

nightclub and a hip roof garden. *84 Pireos St.* ☎ *210/342-5335. Metro: Kerameikos. Map p 113.*

Decadence EXARCHIA   The most popular of a bevy of clubs in student-saturated Exachia occupies a beautiful neoclassical mansion and often hosts live rock groups. *69 Voulgaroktonou St.* ☎ *210/882-7045. Metro: Omonia. Map p 111.*

Casino Action

Greeks love to gamble, and there are two casinos near Athens. **Club Hotel Casino Loutraki** is in the seaside resort town of the same name, 80km (50 miles) south; 48 Poseidonos Ave. (☎ 27440/65-501; www.clubhotelloutraki.gr or www.casinoloutraki.gr). The complex has 80 gaming tables, 1,000 slot machines, a luxury hotel, a restaurant, and a spa. Many older gamblers come to soak in curative hot springs between bouts at the slots. The casino makes transport easy with its own Casino Express bus that makes frequent runs to and from Athens (☎ 210/523-4188 or 210/523-4144); the 20€ fare includes casino entrance, drinks on the gaming floors, and a meal at the Neptune restaurant. The **Regency Casino Mont Parnes,** on Mount Parnitha (☎ 210/242-1234; www.regency.gr) has 53 table games and 508 slot machines. A cable car takes you up to the complex from the base of the mountain in Aharnon in northern Athens (18km/11 miles from central Athens), or you can make the ascent by car (30km/19 miles).

★ **Frame Garden** KOLONAKI A slightly retro ambiance prevails at this stylish lounge that spills off an airy portico into a beautifully lit garden. International music, sometimes live, accompanies a menu of light fare and grown-up cocktails. *St. George Lycabettus Hotel. 78 Kleomenous. ☎ 210/729-0711. www.sglycabettus. gr. May–Oct noon–midnight. AE, DC, MC, V. Bus: 22, 60, or 200. Map p 111.*

★ **45 Degrees** GAZI Bypass the crowded bar downstairs and head straight to the rooftop terrace overlooking the Acropolis—a mellow place to begin or end your nighttime explorations of Gazi and Psyrri. *18 Iakou. ☎ 210/346-0901. Daily 7pm–3am. Metro: Thission. Map p 113.*

★ **Galaxy Bar** HILTON A drink on the top floor of this landmark comes with a gorgeous view of the Acropolis. *Hilton Athens, 46 Vas. Sofias Ave. ☎ 210/728-1000. Metro: Evangelismos. Map p 111.*

★ **Mamacas** GAZI Just as stylish and popular as the restaurant of the same name across the street (see p 105), this simple room that spills onto the street is almost a mandatory stop for those who make the nighttime scene in trendy Gazi. *41 Persefonis St. ☎ 210/346-4984. www.mamacas.gr. Daily 10pm till late (4–5am on weekends). Metro: Kerameikos. Map p 113.*

Mike's Irish Bar AMBELOKIPI An outpost for ex-pats in Athens (with a strong contingent of Americans) serves a decent pint of Guinness and offers all sorts of diversions, from darts to televised soccer matches to karaoke and, on some nights, live rock and funk. *6 Sinopis St. behind Athens Tower. ☎ 210/777-6797. Mon–Fri from 8pm; Sat–Sun from 3pm; closed Aug. Cover 3€ for karaoke night & 6€ for live shows. Metro: Ambelokipi or trolley: 3, 7, 8,* 13 or bus: 230, 408, 419, 450, 550. Map p 111.

Moet & Chandon OMONIA Tired of ouzo and retsina? Take a seat in Athens's only champagne bar and sip bubbly in hip and colorful environs with slightly clubby overtones. *Classic Baby Grand Hotel, Athinas 65. ☎ 210/325-0900. www.classicalhotels.com. Daily 11am–11:30pm. AE, DC, MC, V. Metro: Omonia. Map p 112.*

★ **Nipiagogio** GAZI What is maybe the most talked about club in Gazi (for the moment, at least) occupies a former elementary school (the name means "kindergarten"). *8 Kleanthous St. ☎ 210/345-8534. Daily 10pm till late (6am on weekends). Metro: Kerameikos. Map p 113.*

Periscope KOLONAKI A drink or light meal in the lounge of one of the city's hippest hotels is a sightseeing experience—sofas and chairs are the seats of Morris Minis and tables are Ferrari red and equipped with joysticks that allow you to maneuver panoramic views of the city that spin overhead. *22 Haritos St. ☎ 210/729-7200. www. periscope.gr. 8am–1am. AE, DC, MC,*

Even the sign has an island feel at Mamacas, which attracts a hip crowd with its good but expensive food and packed bar.

Podilato means "bicycle" in Greek, and that's the main feature of this small, easygoing student bar.

V. Metro: Syntagma or bus: 022, 060, 200. Map p 111.

Podilato EXARCHIA   Laid-back, stylishly retro, and perpetually crowded, the "Bicycle" caters largely to chatty students who seem determined to drink and talk until dawn. *48 Themistokleous St.* ☎ *210/330-3430. Metro: Omonia. Map p 111.*

★★★ **Thirio** PSYRRI   You'd have to be pretty thick-skinned not to get in the mood for romance on these two levels divided into little cubbyholes, lit by candles and decorated with African tribal artifacts. For an exotic flourish, get on the dance floor and sway to the tracks of

The avant-garde layout of the T-Palace bar in the King George Palace Hotel was designed by Greek film director Antonis Kalogridis.

world music. *1 Lepeniotou St.* ☎ *210/321-7836. Mon 8:30pm till late; Tues–Sun 3:30pm till late. Metro: Monastiraki. Map p 112.*

T-Palace SYNTAGMA   A sleek modernist lounge in one of the city's best hotels is a stylish place for cocktails on busy Syntagma Square. You may choose to stay and linger over another drink or two when the DJ arrives with a repertoire of Greek and international music. *King George Palace Hotel, 3 Vas. Georgiou St. at Syntagma Sq.* ☎ *210/325-0504. www.classicalhotels.com. Metro: Syntagma. Map p 111.*

Dance Clubs

★ **Booze Cooperativa** SYN-TAGMA   Three floors of an old factory offer a little bit of everything—coffeehouse, bar, dance club, art gallery, screening room, meeting place. Music is often live, and at other times provided by some of the city's most popular DJs. Should you still wish to smoke while clubbing, this is the place to do so as Booze is registered as a political headquarters, exempting it from the ban. *Kolokotroni 27.* ☎ *210/324-0944. www.boozecooperativa.com. Daily noon–late. Metro: Syntagma. Map p 111.*

★ **Envy** PSYRRI   This big mainstream club caters to well-heeled youth, who dance to hip-hop, R&B, and Greek music on Sunday. As do many Athenians, the club moves to the island of Paros in summer. *Monastiraki Center, 3 Agias Eleousis St.* ☎ *210/331-7801 or 210/331-7802. www.dubliner.gr. Daily from midnight. Wed–Thurs & Sun 10€ cover; Fri–Sat 15€. Reservations recommended. Metro: Monastiraki. Map p 112.*

Gallery Club KOLONAKI A slightly older crowd drops in to dance to music that runs the gamut from Greek to disco to Western nostalgia. *17 Amerikis St.* ☎ *210/362-3901. Daily from 10pm. Metro: Syntagma. Map p 111.*

The Hall THISSIO A huge warehouse hosts celebrity DJs from throughout Greece and Europe to play a wide mix of genres to wildly enthusiastic crowds. *1 Asomaton Sq. at Ermou St.* ☎ *210/322-4553. Fri–Sat year-round 11pm–late. Cover from 20€, depending on event. Metro: Thissio. Map p 112.*

Kalua SYNTAGMA One of the city's oldest discos is still going strong, appealing to everyone from visiting businessmen to die-hard dance fans. *6 Amerikis St.* ☎ *210/360-8304. Daily from midnight. 15€ cover. Metro: Syntagma. Map p 111.*

Drink by candlelight at Thirio.

LavaBore ZAPPEION If you're young, restless, and just passing through town, you've found your spot! Dancing is to popular foreign music, though it switches to Greek near closing when Athenians pour in to round off a night of clubbing. *25 Filellinon St.* ☎ *210/324-5335. Daily Feb–Nov; closed Dec–Jan. 10€ cover w/drink. Metro: Syntagma. Map p 112.*

★ **Mad Club** GAZI The favorite place to dance in popular Gazi plays 1980s rock for an enthusiastic crowd that wasn't even born when this music came on the scene. *53 Persefonis St.* ☎ *210/346-2007. Daily from midnight. Cover varies. Metro: Kerameikos. Map p 113.*

Nightlife Districts

It's pretty easy to find a club or bar in Athens. When in doubt, head to **Psyrri**, once a nighttime nest of hooligans and these days *the* place to be for anyone who wants to partake of nightlife. **Gazi** is the city's up-and-coming gay district, with bars and clubs that tend to cater to men and women, straight and gay. Clubs and bars in **Exarchia** are popular with students, not surprisingly, given the presence of Athens University. The pedestrian streets and squares of **Plaka** and **Thissio** are chockablock with outdoor cafes and bars, many with gardens or rooftop terraces and a few with knockout views of the Acropolis.

★ **Pop** MONASTIRAKI   Small and perennially popular, this intimate cocktail lounge serves up a mix of music and a fizzy potent house elixir that keeps the action going all night. *Kleitou 10B.* ☎ *210/322-0650. Daily from 11pm. Metro: Monastiraki. Map p 112.*

Romeo GLYFADA   You can dance until dawn and on the tables at this big music hall on the coast. If you feel you can't keep up, settle for showering the singers and dancers with flowers. *1 Ellinikou St.* ☎ *210/894-5345. Thurs–Sat year-round from 11pm. Tram: Ellinikou Olympionikon. Map p 113.*

★ **Six D.O.G.S.** MONASTIRAKI   Four adjoining bars joined forces to create one of the city's most exciting and hippest venues that combines a laid-back library, sleek cocktail lounge, and huge dance hall/performance space. The design is sleek and minimalist and the music, provided by popular DJs and bands, is enhanced with remarkable acoustics that bring dancers out in force. *Avramiotou 6–8.* ☎ *210/321-0510. www.sixdogs.gr. Daily 10am–late night. Metro: Monastiraki. Map p 112.*

Vanilla Project PSYRRI   A rather glamorous and prosperous crowd enjoys two DJ-manned dance floors

Late-night dancing and partying at Romeo, which serves up live music after-hours.

and a huge bar. *37 Sarri St.* ☎ *210/322-0647. Closed July–Aug. 15€ cover w/ drink. Metro: Monastiraki. Map p 112.*

Venti PSYRRI   An open-air dance floor and Greek pop music is a hit with young Athenians, especially in summer when most other clubs move to the seaside or shut down entirely. *29 Lepiniotou St.* ☎ *210/325-4504. www.venti.gr. Daily year-round from midnight. Metro: Thissio. Map p 112.*

Gay & Lesbian

Aleko's Island PSYRRI   A laid-back island atmosphere is helped along by mellow lounge music. Owner Alekos is usually on hand to greet his regulars and make anyone who walks in the door, straight or gay, feel at home. *41 Sarri St. No phone. Daily from 9pm–3:30am. Metro: Syntagma. Map p 112.*

Lamda MAKRIGIANNI   One of the oldest and most popular gay bars in Athens caters to men; an older clientele relaxes on the main floor, while a younger and rowdier crowd gravitates to the lower level. There are live shows on the weekends. *15 Lembessi St.* ☎ *210/922-4202. www.lamdaclub.gr. Daily from 11pm–5am. Metro: Acropolis. Map p 112.*

Noiz Club GAZI   This big, noisy club offers two dance floors and two DJs and is especially popular with gay women. *41 Evmolpidon St.* ☎ *210/342-4771. www.noizclub.gr. Daily from 11pm. Metro: Thission. Map p 113.*

Sodade GAZI   This bar-club-lounge is a mainstay in the gay-friendly district of Gazi, popular with men and women whatever their tastes might be and packed on weekend nights. *10 Triptolemou St.* ☎ *210/346-8657. www.sodade.gr. 8€ cover. Sun–Thurs 10pm–4am, Fri–Sat 10pm–6am. Metro: Kerameikos. Map p 113.* ●

Arts & Entertainment **Best Bets**

Best **Place to See Greek Folk Dance**
★★ Dora Stratou Theatre, *Filopappou Hill (p 128)*

Best **Place to See an Ancient Play**
★★★ Epidaurus Theater, *Epidavros (p 128)*

Best **Jazz Club**
Half Note Jazz Club, *17 Trivonianou St. (p 131)*

Best **Summer Evening Out**
★★★ Odeon of Herodes Atticus, *Acropolis (p 128)*

Best **Concert Hall**
★ Megaron Mousikis, *Vas. Sofias and Kokkali sts. (p 129)*

Best **Low–Brow Evening Out**
★★ Stamatopoulos, *26 Lissiou St. (p 130)*

Best **Place to See an Avant-Garde Performance**
★★ Technopolis, *100 Piraeos St. (p 131)*

Best **Outdoor Cinema**
★★★ Thission Open–Air Cinema, *7 Apostolou Pavlou St. (p 127)*

Best **Place to See Contemporary Art**
★★ Benaki Museum–Pireos Street, *138 Pireos St. (p 126)*

Best **Place to See a Masterpiece**
★ National Art Gallery & Alexandros Soutzos Museum, *60 Vas. Konstantinou St. (p 127)*

Best **Intimate Venue for a Classical Concert**
★ Athenaeum International Cultural Centre, *3 Adrianou St. (p 128)*

This page: Ballet choreographed by Maurice Béjart at the Herodes Atticus Theater.
Previous page: A performer represents the ancient Greek muse of theater at the opening ceremony of the Athens 2004 Olympic Games.

Gazi, Psyrri & Koukaki A&E

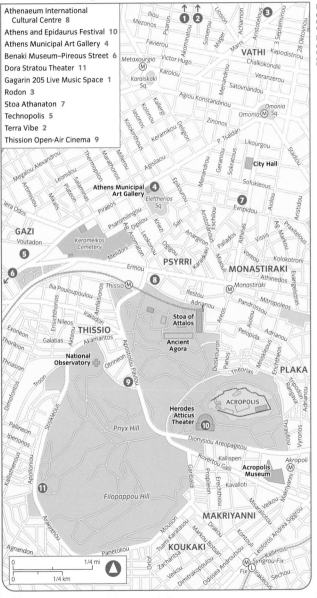

Plaka & Makriyanni A&E

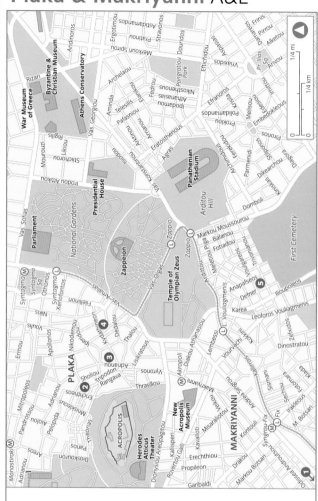

Cine Paris **3**
Frissiras Museum **4**
Half Note Jazz Club **5**
New Eugenides
Planetarium **1**
Stamatopoulos **2**

Lycabettus A&E

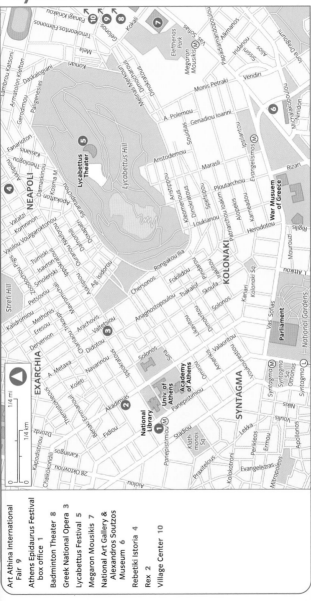

Arts & Entertainment A to Z

Art

Art Athina International Fair
FALIRO Connoisseurs from all over the world come to Athens in mid–May to see the latest in contemporary art from Greek and European artists. The funny, thought-provoking, and avant-garde work—much of which is for sale—includes paintings, installations, sculpture, video art, and photography. The Faliro Pavilion, a former Olympic venue at 2 Moraitini St., hosts the fair. *140 Solonos St.* ☎ *210/330-3355. www.art-athina.gr. Tram: Red line from Syntagma to Delta Falirou. Map p 125.*

Athens Municipal Art Gallery
KOUMOUNDOUROU The emphasis in the city's art museum is on work by 20th-century Greek artists, but also fascinating are drawings and plans by Ernst Ziller, the German architect who designed many of the neoclassical mansions and municipal buildings that transformed Athens in the 19th century. The gallery is housed not in one of Ziller's buildings but in a former factory designed by one of his colleagues, the Danish architect Hans Christian Hansen, who also designed the Senate of the University of Athens (see the "Architectural Athens" tour, p 44). Frequent temporary exhibitions often include showings of some of Greece's outstanding private art collections. *Mylierou 32.* ☎ *210/324-3023. Mon–Fri 9am–1pm & 5–9pm; Sun 9am–1pm. Free admission. Metro: Thissio or Omonia. Map p 123.*

★★ Benaki Museum–Pireos Street THISSIO The Benaki's stunning outpost in an industrial sector is well worth a visit just to enjoy the airy and bold expanses of glass and stone. The high-ceilinged, multilevel galleries host many temporary exhibitions on architecture, photography, contemporary sculpture, and other genres that present some of the capital's most exciting art. *138 Pireos St.* ☎ *210/345-3111. www.benaki.gr. Wed–Thurs, Sun 10am–6pm; Fri–Sat 10am–10pm. Admission 6€; 3€ seniors and students. Metro: Kerameikos. Map p 123.*

Visitors to the National Art Gallery & Alexandros Soutzos Museum view an exhibition on Colombian artist Fernando Botero.

Frissiras Museum PLAKA A permanent collection of 20th-century and contemporary European art is spread throughout two 19th-century houses, and the museum usually has one or two special exhibitions on view as well. The subject matter is almost always cutting edge, showcasing the latest in European digital, video, and graphic arts. *3 & 7 Monis Asteriou St.* ☎ *210/323-4678. www.frissirasmuseum.com. Wed–Fri 10am–5pm; Sat–Sun 11am–5pm. Tickets 6€; 3€ seniors and students. Metro: Syntagma. Map p 124.*

★ **National Art Gallery & Alexandros Soutzos Museum** HILTON A small but worthy collection includes Renaissance paintings, works by El Greco, and Byzantine icons, much of it donated by Alexander Soutzos half a century ago. The museum also hosts some blockbuster traveling exhibitions; if a world-renowned show of 16th-century Dutch art or French Impressionism comes to Athens, the National Art Gallery will probably be the host. *60 Vas. Konstantinou St.* ☎ *210/723-5937. www.nationalgallery.gr. Mon & Wed–Sat 9am–3pm; Sun 10am–2pm. Tickets 6.50€; 3€ children 12–18; free for 11 & under. Metro: Evangelismos. Map p 125.*

Cinema

★★★ **Cine Paris** PLAKA Even if a film isn't screening, step off Plaka's main square to see the reproductions of old Greek movie posters. At showtime, head upstairs to the roof garden, where films (mostly English-language hits with Greek subtitles) are screened under the stars. Here and at the capital's other open-air cinemas movies are shown June to August, with two nightly screenings that usually begin at 9pm and later. Though open-air cinemas are going the way of the American drive-in, those that remain are beloved and

One of the city's many open-air cinemas.

popular. Don't expect to be surrounded by reverent filmgoers: The chance to sit outdoors and socialize on a summer night is often as much of an attraction as the film. *22 Kydathineon St.* ☎ *210/322–2071. Tickets 7€. Metro: Syntagma. Map p 124.*

★ **kids New Eugenides Planetarium** AMPHITHEA The Athens planetarium is one of the most advanced in the world, using ramped-up IMAX technology to screen spectacular journeys into space and beneath the sea on a giant sky dome. *Eugenides Institute, 387 Syngrou.* ☎ *210/946-9600. www.eugenfound.edu.gr. Adults 8€, children & students 5€. Bus: 126, B2, A2 (from Akadimias St.), 550. Map p 124.*

★★★ **Thission Open-Air Cinema** THISSIO Views of the Acropolis steal the show at this beloved institution just off the Grand Promenade. Retro films, many in English with Greek subtitles, are often on the bill. *7 Apostolou Pavlou St.* ☎ *210/347-0980. Tickets 7€. Metro: Thissio. Map p 123.*

Village Center MAROUSSI One of Athens's largest multiplex theaters shows American blockbusters on many of its 14 screens. Make a night of it and get in a game or two at the bowling alley next door. *Frangoklissias St.* ☎ *210/610-5950.*

The ancient Epidaurus outdoor theater can seat 15,000 spectators.

www.villagecinemas.gr. *Metro: Maroussi. Map p 125.*

Classical Music, Opera & Dance

★ **Athenaeum International Cultural Centre** THISSIO The Athenaeum is dedicated to Greek-American opera legend Maria Callas, with the mission of promoting music in Greece; it sponsors many classical concerts, including a winter and spring series at the center's neoclassical headquarters. The Maria Callas Grand Prix international competition for operatic vocalists and pianists brings international talent to the city in March, and the annual September 16 commemorative concert on the anniversary of the singer's death, staged at the Odeon of Herodus Atticus, is one of the city's big events. *3 Adrianou St.* ☎ *210/321-1987. www.athenaeum.com.gr. Tickets 10€; 5€ students. Metro: Thissio or Monastiraki. Map p 123.*

★★★ **Athens and Epidaurus Festival** PANEPISTIMIOU Athens's biggest performing arts event brings drama, opera, symphonies, ballet, and modern dance to venues throughout Athens. Audiences come from all over the world to see dazzling performances by an international roster of stars. The **Odeon of Herodes Atticus** (☎ **210/324-2121** or 210/323-2771) hosts many of the performances, and the sight of the Acropolis looming overhead is no small part of the spectacle. The remarkably well-preserved **Epidaurus Theater** stages many of the festival's productions of classical drama; Epidaurus is about 2 hours south of Athens, and packages that include transport by bus are available. Tickets for events run from 15€ to 100€ and go on sale about 2 weeks in advance. *Box office: 39 Panepistimiou St.* ☎ *210/327-2000. www.greekfestival.gr. May–Oct. Ticket prices vary. Metro: Panepistimiou. Map p 123.*

★★ **Dora Stratou Theatre** FILOPAPPOU The Dora Stratou troupe, a beloved Athenian institution, has been performing traditional Greek folk dances at a beautiful theater on Filopappou Hill since 1953. *Box office: 8 Scholiou St.* ☎ *210/324-4395. Theater: Filopappou Hill.* ☎ *210/921-4650. www.grdance.org. Performances: May–Sept Tues–Sat at 9:30pm; Sun at 8:15pm. Ticket office: 9am–4pm; 7:30–9pm before performances. Tickets 15€–25€. Metro: Petralona or bus/trolley: 15, 227. Map p 123.*

A *Bouzoukia* Night

Bouzoukia music is still popular in Greece and is played at tavernas and clubs around the city. For a sampling of a few, you can go on an organized tour that includes dinner and dancing. Some of the better-known tour operators are **CHAT Tours,** 4 Stadiou St. (☎ 210/322-3137 or 322-3886), and **Key Tours,** 4 Kallirois St. (☎ 210/923-3166; www.keytours.gr); both offer "Athens by Night" tours for about 100€ (including dinner). If you venture out on your own, keep in mind that in the big *bouzoukia* clubs a bottle of whiskey can set you back 100€ or more; try to stand at the bar, where you can get a drink for about 15€. Remember, too, that smashing plates is a thing of the past—today's fans throw flowers at their favorite performers.

The bouzouki was the precursor of the lute and is a staple of rebetika music.

Greek National Opera OMONIA
The **Olympia Theatre** hosts the company's September to June season, and a few performances are staged in the summer at the Odeon of **Herodes Atticus** as part of the Athens and Epidaurus Festival (see above). The company also mounts productions for children, mostly at the **Akropol Theatre.** *Olympia Theatre: 59–61 Akademias St. ☎ 210/364-3725. Akropol: 9–11 Ippokratous St. ☎ 210/364–3700. www.nationalopera.gr. Box office daily 9am–9pm. Ticket prices vary. Metro: Omonia. Map p 125.*

★ **Megaron Mousikis** EMBASSY
Exceptionally fine acoustics make this modern concert hall a standout on the classical musical circuit, and recitals, symphonic performances, and other programs by an international roster of musical talent run from September to June. *Vas. Sofias & Kokkali sts. ☎ 210/729-0391 or 210/728-2333. Central ticket kiosk: 1 Ermou St. ☎ 210/324-3297. www.megaron.gr. Box office: Mon–Fri 10am–6pm; Sat 10am–2pm; longer*

on performance nights, including Sun 6–8:30pm. Kiosk: Mon–Fri 10am–6pm. Tickets 14€–100€. Metro: Megaron Mousikis. Map p 125.

Dinner Shows
Rebetiki Istoria NEAPOLI
Rebetika, the Greek equivalent of blues, originated with the underclasses in the 1920s and 1930s and is a popular fixture of the club scene.

Megaron Mousikis is the city's modern concert hall.

Who's Playing

To keep up to date on Athens's lively schedule of music, films, and dance, check the entertainment listings in English-language magazines such as **Athens News** (www.athensnews.gr), published in print on Fridays, and the daily Greek news insert in the **International Herald Tribune.** For rock and popular music concerts, log onto **www.rockpages.gr** (with an English version). If you wish to attend the very popular performances of the Athens and Epidaurus Festival or the Lycabettus Festival, stop by the Hellenic Festival Box Office (39 Panepistimiou St., ☎ 210/928-2900, Mon–Fri 8:30am–4pm, Sat 9am–2:30pm); the office has info on many festivals around Greece. Other good online sources for information on performing arts and events in Athens are www.athensinfoguide.com and www.greektourism.com.

Tickets can be bought through organizers, promoters, venues, ticket agents, and some record stores, such as **Metropolis,** 64 and 54 Panepistimiou St. (☎ 210/380-8549; www.metropolis.gr). **Ticketnet,** 46 Kifissias Ave. (☎ 210/884-0600; www.ticketnet.gr); **Ticket House,** 42 Panepistimiou St. (☎ 210/360-8366; www.tickethouse.gr); and **Ticket Shop** (☎ 210/336-2888; www.ticketshop.gr) also list and sell tickets for Athens venues.

This smoky lair is one of the most popular of the many *rebetika* clubs around the city and attracts a crowd of older regulars and enthusiastic students. *181 Ippokratous St. ☎ 210/642-4937. Sept–Easter Tues–Sun; June Fri–Sat only; closed July–Aug. Cover 6€ includes first drink. Bus: 230. Map p 125.*

Rex SYNTAGMA With its laser lights, Vegas-style staging, and big name entertainers, this flashy place is probably not what comes to mind when you think of old-fashioned Greek music. But *bouzoukia* was once served up with a lot more pizzazz than it is now, and this is one of the few remaining big clubs that keep the tradition alive. *48 Panepistimiou St. ☎ 210/381-4591. Daily 7pm–2am; closed July–Aug. Metro: Syntagma. Map p 125.*

★★ **Stamatopoulos** PLAKA
Wall murals re-creating life in early-20th-century Athens set the mood for a night of fine traditional *rebetika* and *bouzoukia* music, accompanied by good taverna fare and decent house wine. *26 Lissiou St. at Flessa St. ☎ 210/322-8722. www.stamatopoulostavern.gr. Daily 7pm–2am. Metro: Syntagma. Map p 124.*

★★ **Stoa Athanaton** OMONIA
Many *rebetika* legends show up regularly to perform at this storied old 1930s club tucked away in the Central Market. A late lunch crowd can get their *rebetika* fix at matinee sessions from 3:30–7:30pm. *Sofokleous 19, Central Market. Lissiou St. at Flessa St. ☎ 210/321-4362. Mon–Sat noon–2am. Metro: Omonia. Map p 123.*

Jazz

Half Note Jazz Club METS The city's most popular venue for jazz has hosted the greats for the past 30 years. *17 Trivonianou St.* ☎ *210/921-3310. www.halfnote.gr. Tues–Sat 10:30pm till late; Sun–Mon 8:30pm till late. Tickets: 30€ including first drink; tables 35€ or 40€. Bus: A3, B3, 057. Map p 124.*

Popular Music

Gagarin 205 Live Music Space THYMARAKIA This large hall hosts a rock concert almost every night, with a lineup of Greek and international stars playing to crowds of 1,300 or more. Check the website to see who's performing, and in the summer, where, come June, the action moves to various Gagarin venues on the coast. *205 Liosion Ave.* ☎ *210/854-7601. www.gagarin205. gr. Metro: Attikis. Map p 123.*

Lycabettus Festival KOLONAKI The outdoor theater atop Lycabettus Hill is another magical Athenian setting for summertime concerts of popular music. Bob Dylan, Diana Ross, and scores of other international stars have been headliners. *Theater:* ☎ *210/722-7233; Box office*

is same as for Athens and Epidaurus Festival (see p 128): *39 Panepistimiou St.* ☎ *210/327-2000. www. greekfestival.gr. May–Oct. Ticket prices vary. Metro: Panepistimiou. Map p 125.*

Rodon OMONIA Some of the biggest names in rock have appeared at this big club since it opened in the 1980s—in fact, Rodon basically brought rock and pop to Athens in the era when the city was just emerging from the era of military rule. Local and foreign acts that have made it to the pop charts still make regular appearances. *24 Marni St.* ☎ *210/524-7427. Metro: Omonia. Map p 123.*

★★ Technopolis GAZI A fume-spewing factory is now Athens's trendiest art center. Technopolis is a "City of Art," and huge spaces in the six main halls of the 30-acre complex house an ever-changing roster of temporary art exhibits. These often highlight the work of young Greek artists, displayed against a backdrop of discarded furnaces and equipment. The complex is also the dramatic backdrop for cutting-edge concerts and dance performances. In the first 2 weeks of July, Technopolis hosts

The Half Note Jazz Club, across from the First Cemetery, has been around for more than 30 years.

The Badminton Theater hosts internationally renowned performances.

the Athens International Dance Festival, with performances by modern-dance companies from

throughout the world. *100 Piraeos St. at Persefonis St.* ☎ *210/346-1589 or 210/346-7322. Metro: Kerameikos. Map p 123.*

Terra Vibe MALAKASA   This outdoor arena for big name pop and rock acts is best known as the home of the annual multiday Rockwave Festival in July, with a slew of famous musicians. *Lamia National Rd. at Malakasa junction.* ☎ *210/882-0426. www.didimusic.gr. Tickets: www. tickethouse.gr. Tickets from 40€. Train: Sfendali Station. Map p 123.*

Theater
★ kids **Badminton Theater** GOUDI   This 2,500-seat former Olympic venue hosts big musical acts and traveling shows such as *Mamma Mia!* and *Lion King* when they come to Athens. *Kannelopoulou Ave.* ☎ *211/101-0020. www. badmintontheater.gr. Tickets: www. ticketnet.gr. Ticket prices vary. Metro: Katehaki. Map p 125.* ●

For the Sports Fan

The Greeks are fiercely devoted to sport, with football (soccer) and basketball topping the list. **Panathinaikos FC** (☎ 801/111-1908; www.ticketclub.gr) and **Olympiakos Piraeus** (☎ 210/414-3000; www.olympiakos.gr) are the nation's intensely rivalrous football squads and often meet at Olympiakos's **Karaiskaki Stadium** (☎ 210/480-0900; www.karaiskaki.gr) to compete. **AEK** also plays in Athens at the distinctive Calatrava-designed **Olympic Athletic Center of Athens** (☎ 210/683-4060; www.oaka.com.gr).

The **Athens Race Track** at Markopolou (☎ 22990/81-000) is a good spot to witness the national passion for horse racing and betting.

Golf is gaining popularity in Greece, and one of the nicest courses near Athens is the **Glyfada Club,** on the coast at Terma Pronois Street (☎ 210/894-6459; www.ggca.gr). A round at this challenging 18-hole resort starts at about 50€.

9 The Best **Lodging**

Lodging **Best Bets**

Best **Large Luxury Hotel**
★ Athenaeum Intercontinental
$$$ 89–93 Syngrou Ave. (p 139)

Best **Hostel**
Student & Travellers Inn $
16 Kydathineon St. (p 146)

Best **Budget Lodging for Families**
★★ Athens Studios $ 3A Veikou St. (p 140)

Best **Hotel in the Plaka**
★★★ Electra Palace $$$
18 Nikodimou St. (p 141)

Best **Trendy Hotel**
★ Eridanus $$$ 78 Pireos St. (p 141)

Best **Old-World Luxury Hotel**
★★★ Grande Bretagne $$$$
Syntagma Sq. (p 142)

Best **Hotel near the Acropolis**
★★ Herodion Hotel $$ 4 Rovertou Galli St. (p 143)

Best **Quiet Hotel near the Acropolis**
★ Acropolis View Hotel $
10 Webster St. (p 138)

Best **Nice Hotel in a Great Location**
★★ St. George Lycabettus $$$
78 Kleomenous (p 146)

Best **Budget Hotels with Acropolis Views**
★ Hotel Attalos $ 29 Athinas St. (p 144); and ★ Adonis Hotel $ 3 Kodrou St. (p 138)

Best **Intimate Getaway**
★ Ochre & Brown $$$ 7 Leokoriou St. (p 145)

Best **Contemporary Design**
★ Semiramis $$$ 48 Harialou St. (p 146)

Best **for in-City Resort Feeling**
★ Meliá Athens $$ 28 Octovriou St. (p 145)

Best **Seaside Getaway**
★ Grand Resort Lagonissi $$$$
Athens–Sounion Rd. (p 142)

Best **Hotel for Historic Ambience**
★★ Art Hotel Athens $$ 27 Marni St. (p 139)

This page: The pool of the Athenaeum Intercontinental.
Previous page: The Winter Garden, a cafe in the lobby of the Grande Bretagne, has an elegant stained-glass ceiling.

135

Makriyanni & Koukaki Lodging

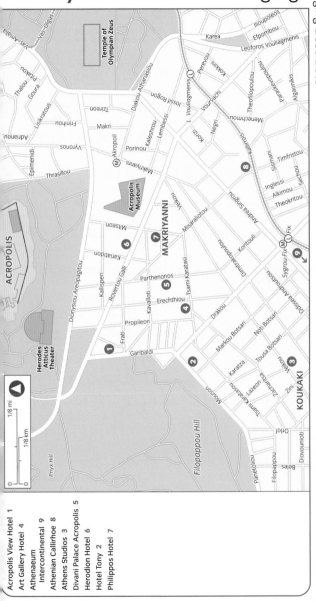

Acropolis View Hotel 1
Art Gallery Hotel 4
Athenaeum
Intercontinental 9
Athenian Callirhoe 8
Athens Studios 3
Divani Palace Acropolis 5
Herodion Hotel 6
Hotel Tony 2
Philippos Hotel 7

The Best Lodging

Omonia, Psyrri, Monastiraki & Plaka Lodging

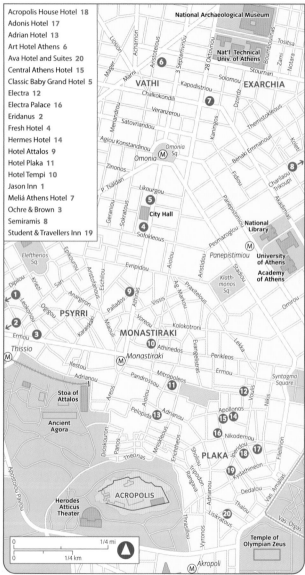

Syntagma & Kolonaki
Lodging

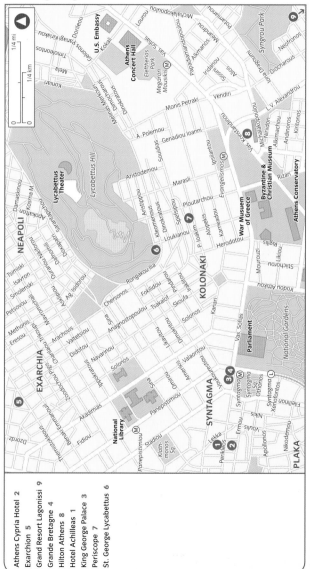

Athens Cypria Hotel 2
Exarchion 5
Grand Resort Lagonissi 9
Grande Bretagne 4
Hilton Athens 8
Hotel Achilleas 1
King George Palace 3
Periscope 7
St. George Lycabettus 6

Athens Lodging A to Z

Acropolis House Hotel PLAKA
One of a string of basic but clean
lodgings in a quiet corner of the
Plaka occupies a 150-year-old villa
and has a bit more character than
its neighbors. Be sure to ask for one
of the older rooms when booking—
those in a newer wing are bland and
the bathrooms, though private, are
across the hall. *6–8 Kodrou St.*
☎ *210/322-2344. www.acropolis
house.gr. 25 units. Doubles 50€–
87€ w/breakfast. MC, V only to
reserve (pay in cash). Metro: Syntagma. Map p 136.*

★ **Acropolis View Hotel** KOU-
KAKI The neighborhood around
this pleasant little inn on the south
side of the Filapappou Hill is leafy
and quiet yet an easy walk away
from Plaka and the ancient sights.
Rooms are fresh and spotless, and
some face the Acropolis, as does
the delightful roof terrace. *10 Webster St. at Rovertou Galli St.* ☎ *210/
921-7303 or 210/921-7305. www.
acropolisview.gr. 32 units. Doubles*

*The simple unadorned roof of the Adonis
Hotel has a charming view of backstreet
Plaka and the Acropolis.*

*80€–100€ w/breakfast. MC, V.
Metro: Akropoli or Syngrou-Fix or
bus/trolley: 1, 5, 15, 230. Map p 135.*

★ **Adonis Hotel** PLAKA Room
decor at this basic, value-for-money
fixture in Plaka doesn't go much
beyond a bed and chair, but for
those on a tight budget the location
(on a pleasant back street just a
10-minute walk from Syntagma Sq.)
and an airy roof terrace may well
compensate for the lack of luxury.
3 Kodrou St. ☎ *210/324-9737. www.
hotel-adonis.gr. 26 units. Doubles
62€–92€ w/breakfast. No credit
cards, except to reserve. Metro:
Syntagma. Map p 136.*

★ **Adrian Hotel** PLAKA One of
the plain rooms here puts you right
in the heart of the Plaka, across the
street from the Roman Forum and
Tower of the Winds. You can see
the ruins and the Acropolis looming
above them from many of the balconies and the roof garden, where
breakfast and drinks are served.
74 Adrianou St. ☎ *210/322-1553.
www.douros-hotels.com. 22 units.
Doubles 82€–150€ w/breakfast. MC,
V. Metro: Monastiraki. Map p 136.*

★ **Art Gallery Hotel** KOUKAKI
A 1950s house beneath Filopappou
Hill was once the residence of artists, who left many of their works
behind. Many guests settle in for
months at a time, and the hardwood
floors and polished old furniture
have a homey lived-in sheen to
them. A buffet breakfast is served in
a top-floor lounge and roof garden
with views of the Acropolis. *5 Erech-
thiou St.* ☎ *210/923-8376. www.art
galleryhotel.gr. 21 units. Doubles
70€–100€. No credit cards. Metro:
Syngrou-Fix or bus/trolley: 1, 5, 15,
230. Map p 135.*

★★ **Art Hotel Athens** OMONIA
A beauty inside and out, this neo-classical 19th-century landmark has been lovingly restored. Lounges show off some stunning contemporary design, but the large, handsome rooms retain their original wooden floors, high ceilings, and huge windows. The surrounding streets can be a bit dodgy at night, but lively Omonia Square and the National Archaeological Museum are just a short walk away. *27 Marni St.* ☎ *210/325-5301. www.arthotel athens.gr. 30 units. Doubles 85€–150€. AE, DC, MC, V. Metro: Omonia. Map p 136.*

A room at the Adrian in Plaka.

★ **kids Athenaeum Intercontinental** NEOS KOSMOS Visiting dignitaries and celebs often stay at Athens's largest luxury hotel, where the extremely comfortable and attractive rooms are oversized and the many amenities include a pool—making this a popular choice for families, too. The bland neighborhood is geared to business, but the Plaka is a short Metro ride or 15-minute walk away. *89–93 Syngrou Ave.* ☎ *210/920-6000. www.intercontinental.com. 543 units.*

Lodging Tips

Athens supplies travelers with a huge selection of hotels, and the hotel scene has gotten bigger and better in the past decade after getting a big boost from the 2004 Olympics. This bumper crop of new rooms has been a boon for travelers, who can usually find some excellent deals in the post-Olympics era—all the more so since economic woes at home and abroad have put a damper on the city's tourism industry. To find the best prices, check out hotel websites. Also look for special offers: 3 nights for the price of 2; 20 percent discount for stays of a week; special room, dinner, and sightseeing packages—hoteliers are creative in their offers, much to your benefit. Concepts of low and high seasons are a bit murky in Athens; summer is low season for many business-oriented hotels, and some woo the family trade with good prices, but summer is high season for tourist-oriented hotels, where prices might plunge in the winter months. When in doubt, ask, and bargain—if rooms are available, savvy hoteliers will be happy to negotiate. Wherever you stay, room rates usually include taxes and breakfast, which in many cases is a lavish buffet. And remember—some hotels, especially in the budget category, accept only cash or will give you a discount if you pay in cash.

Roomy quarters have kitchenettes at Athens Studios.

Doubles 230€–260€. AE, DC, MC, V. Metro: Syngrou-Fix or bus/trolley: A2, B2, E2, E22, 9, 040, 126, 450, 550, or tram: Neos Kosmos. Map p 135.

Athenian Callirhoe MAKRIYANNI This very stylish retreat is in a business district but within reach of the major sights—in exchange for being a bit removed from the center of things, you can enjoy oversized guest rooms and suites, a stunning bar and rooftop restaurant, and pampering touches that include a sauna. Sound-proofing keeps traffic noise from the surrounding avenues at bay. *32 Kallirois Ave.* ☎ *210/921-5353. www. tac.gr. 84 units. Doubles 150€–170€ w/breakfast. AE, DC, MC, V. Metro: Akropoli or tram: Fix. Map p 135.*

Athens Cypria Hotel SYNTAGMA During the summer, this popular business hotel just off Syntagma Square turns its attention to families, offering discounts for kids, reasonable rates for connecting rooms and junior suites, and a generous buffet breakfast. The car-free square and nearby National Gardens are handy for letting the little ones run off steam. *5 Diomias St.* ☎ *210/323-8034 or 210/323-0470. www.athenscypria. com. 124 units. Doubles 119€–129€ w/breakfast. AE, MC, V. Metro: Syntagma. Map p 137.*

★★ kids **Athens Studios** MAKRIYANNI These spacious apartments, with decent kitchens, plenty of space, and spiffy contemporary furnishings, are a big hit with families, and so is the self-service laundry downstairs. The Acropolis is just a few steps away. *3A Veikou St.* ☎ *210/923-5811. www.athensstudios.gr. 35 units. Apt for 2–3 people 70€–120€. MC, V. Metro: Akropoli. Map p 135.*

★ kids **Ava Hotel and Suites** PLAKA All of these spacious units are extremely well-appointed and arranged, with living areas, kitchens, and bedrooms, and they sleep up to four. Flatscreens and other high-end amenities are plentiful. Special rates for stays of a month or longer are available. *9–11 Lyssikratous St.* ☎ *210/325-9000. www. avahotel.gr. 15 units. 250€–330€ w/breakfast. AE, MC, V. Metro: Akropoli. Map p 136.*

★ **Central Athens Hotel** SYNTAGMA Very attractive decor, attentive service, a roof garden with a hot tub, and a prime location add up to excellent value. Many rooms have pullout beds, and some are interconnecting to accommodate families. *21 Apollonos St.* ☎ *210/323-4357. www.centralhotel.gr. 84 units. Doubles 99€–121€ w/breakfast.*

AE, DC, MC, V. Metro: Syntagma. Map p 136.

★ Classic BabyGrand Hotel

OMONIA   Each room is a work of art, decorated with graffiti-like depictions of flowers, birds, trees, clouds, superheroes—not a good choice for those requiring Zen-like surroundings, though some of those, bathed in neutral tones, are available, too. *Athinas 65.* ☎ *210/ 325-0900. www.classicalhotels.com. 75 units. Doubles from 75€. AE, DC, MC, V. Metro: Omonia. Map p 136.*

Divani Palace Acropolis MAKRI-

YANNI   This large hotel just a few blocks south of the Acropolis caters to groups but welcomes independent travelers and offers many amenities not usually available in central Athens—including an outdoor swimming pool and larger than average rooms, all with balconies. An extensive breakfast buffet is served in the rooftop restaurant. *19–25 Parthenonos St.* ☎ *210/928-0100. www. divanis.gr. 253 units. Doubles 143€– 240€ w/breakfast. AE, DC, MC, V. Metro: Syngrou-Fix. Map p 135.*

Electra PLAKA

While not as glamorous as its sibling down the street, the Electra is one of the Plaka's nicest hotels. Rooms are large and extremely comfortable, and the Acropolis and other city-center sights are an easy walk away. *5 Ermou St.* ☎ *210/337-8000. www.electrahotels.gr. 109 units. Doubles 125€–175€ w/breakfast. AE, DC, MC, V. Metro: Syntagma. Map p 136.*

★★★ Electra Palace PLAKA

One of the largest hotels in the Plaka is also the most luxurious. Guest rooms are large and stylishly furnished, with beautiful marble bathrooms, and many have views of the Parthenon. Service is top notch, a lavish buffet breakfast is served in a lovely garden in good weather, and you can see the Acropolis while doing laps in the beautiful rooftop pool. *18 Nikodimou St.* ☎ *210/324-1401 or 210/337-0000. www.electra hotels.gr. 155 units. Doubles 180€– 360€ w/breakfast. AE, DC, MC, V. Metro: Syntagma. Map p 136.*

★ Eridanus GAZI

It only figures that trendy Gazi should have a hip hotel, and here it is, with beautiful guest rooms and lounges full of contemporary flair and the occasional antique or old textile tastefully thrown in. Practical needs are looked after with such touches as in-room fridges, and the in-house restaurant is excellent. *78 Pireos St.* ☎ *210/520-5360.*

A view of the Parthenon from the Divani Palace Acropolis.

www.eridanus.gr. 38 units. Doubles 195€–230€. AE, DC, MC, V. Metro: Kerameikos. Map p 136.

Exarchion EXARCHIA Students and those who still travel like one swarm to this worn but homey outpost in the city's bohemian university quarter. Some nice touches are a bar that spills out onto an arcade out front and a roof terrace. Best of all for many guests, the National Archaeological Museum is just down the street. *78 Kleomenous.* ☎ *210/ 380-0731. www.exarchion.com. 49 units. Doubles 55€–60€. AE, DC, MC, V. Metro: Omonia. Map p 137.*

★ **Fresh Hotel** OMONIA Soothing minimalist design, along with a rooftop pool, sun deck, and Zen-like spa, put a fresh face on the gritty Omonia neighborhood. The youthful staff is helpful, the in-house bar/ restaurants are appealing and serve light Mediterranean fare, and the laid-back ambiance is soothing. When you are adequately recharged and ready to hit the streets, the lively Central Market and hip Psyrri are nearby. *26 Sofokleous St. at Kleisthenous St.* ☎ *210/524-8511. www. freshhotel.gr. 133 units. Doubles 155€–175€ w/breakfast. AE, DC, MC, V. Metro: Omonia. Map p 136.*

The Air Lounge roof bar at Fresh Hotel serves coffee, light lunch, finger food, dinner, and cocktails.

The Electra Palace Garden.

★★★ **Grande Bretagne** SYNTAGMA An Athens landmark for 160 years has housed royalty, celebrities, and world leaders and is still the best address in town. Enough opulence remains to let you know the place has a lineage, yet 21st-century innovations ensure maximum comforts. An attentive staff looks after every detail, and the rooftop pool and adjoining bar restaurant enjoy knockout views of the Acropolis. *Syntagma Sq.* ☎ *210/333-0000. www.grandebretagne.gr. 321 units. Doubles 317€–611€. AE, DC, MC, V. Metro: Syntagma. Map p 137.*

★ **Grand Resort Lagonissi** LAGONISSI Combining a seaside getaway with city sightseeing is easy to do from this stunning luxury complex on the coast about 40 minutes outside the center (buses stop just outside the gates). Sandy beaches, a lovely pool, and accommodations that range from hotel rooms to beachfront bungalows and suites with private pools can put a nice spin on a summertime visit to Athens. *Athens–Sounion Rd.* ☎ *22910/ 76-010. www.grandresort.gr. 370 units. Doubles 350€–500€. AE, DC, MC, V. Bus: KTEL from Aigyptou Sq. Map p 137.*

★ Hermes Hotel PLAKA
The Plaka is chockablock with medium-sized, moderately priced tourist oriented hotels like this but few are as refreshing. Lounges and the airy guest rooms (many with balconies) are well done in an attractive contemporary design, and amenities include a roof terrace, a bar, and a travel desk to help you plan excursions. *19 Apollonos St.* ☎ *210/323-5514 or 210/322-2706. www.hermeshotel.gr. 45 units. Doubles 89€–135€ w/breakfast. AE, DC, MC, V. Metro: Syntagma. Map p 136.*

★★ Herodion Hotel MAKRIYANNI
Everything about this contemporarily styled hotel seems geared to relaxation: The location just down the street from the Odeon of Herodes Atticus is quiet, guest rooms are soothing, you can end a day of sightseeing with a soak in the rooftop Jacuzzi, and the in-house atrium restaurant and bar is a godsend when you're just not up to venturing out for a meal. *4 Rovertou Galli St.* ☎ *210/ 923-6832. www.herodion.gr. 90 units. Doubles 130€–170€. AE, DC, MC, V. Metro: Akropoli. Map p 135.*

★ Hilton Athens KOLONAKI   The 1963 landmark that was once the latest word in a modern Athens hotel

The beaux-arts lobby of the Grande Bretagne has vaulted ceilings, mosaic floors, and Persian carpets.

has plenty of competition these days but holds it own with updated and stylish rooms, gorgeous bathrooms, a wonderful rooftop bar (see p 117), and a huge swimming pool. The 1930s mural on the facade is a beloved fixture on the city scene. *46 Vas. Sofias Ave.* ☎ *210/728-1000. www.athens.hilton.com. 523 units. Doubles 217€–428€ w/breakfast. AE, DC, MC, V. Metro: Evangelismos. Map p 137.*

Hotel Achilleas SYNTAGMA
A bit of design flair goes a long way in placing yet another moderately

Guest rooms at the Hilton Athens have high-speed Internet, mountain or Acropolis views, and marble bathrooms with a bathtub and walk-in shower.

priced Plaka lodging leagues above the competition. The staff is genuinely hospitable, and the pleasant courtyard is a welcome retreat from the busy surroundings. *21 Lekka St. ☎ 210/323-3197. www.achilleas hotel.gr. 34 units. Doubles 80€–135€ w/breakfast. AE, MC, V. Metro: Syntagma. Map p 137.*

★ **Hotel Attalos** MONASTIRAKI A popular fixture on lively Athinas Street offers some of the best value in central Athens. About half of the basic but attractive rooms have balconies, and some overlook the Acropolis, as does the roof-terrace. Keep in mind, though, that you are likely to encounter drugs, prostitution, and plenty of nighttime rowdiness in the surrounding area. *29 Athinas St. ☎ 210/321-2801. www. attaloshotel.com. 80 units. Doubles 50€–85€. AE, MC, V. Metro: Monastiraki. Map p 136.*

Hotel Plaka MONASTIRAKI Most of the calm, handsome guest rooms enjoy views of the Acropolis or across the Plaka to Lycabettus Hill. The roof-terrace bar is an oasis of calm above the shop-lined streets below. *7 Kapnikareas St. at Mitropoleos St. ☎ 210/322-2096. www. plakahotel.gr. 67 units. Doubles 95€–135€ w/breakfast. AE, DC, MC, V. Metro: Monastiraki or bus: 025, 026, 027. Map p 136.*

Hotel Tempi MONASTIRAKI Location and budget are the big (and some would say only) draws at this barebones hotel facing the church of Ayia Irini and its flower market. The very basic rooms are clean and guests have use of a communal kitchen. *29 Aiolou St. ☎ 210/ 321-3175. www.tempihotel.gr. 24 units. Doubles 45€–64€. AE, MC, V. Metro: Monastiraki. Map p 136.*

The Hotel Scene

Any of the city center hotels put you within easy reach of the sights you'll want to see, but "city center" covers a lot of neighborhoods in sprawling Athens. Many travelers head straight to the Plaka, right in the thick of things between the Acropolis and Syntagma Square. Time was, the Plaka was chockablock with hostels and budget hotels. Many of these budget choices have been spruced up in recent years and now provide clean accommodations and a few amenities (including air-conditioning) at reasonable prices. The Filopappou and Koukaki neighborhoods, just to the south of the Acropolis, are convenient but much quieter than the Plaka (and for those who enjoy being in the thick of cafes and nightlife, quite a bit duller). Some of the city's most exciting new hotels are sprouting up on unlikely turf around gritty Omonia. While the traffic-clogged avenues and forlorn side streets of this central business district may be off-putting to some travelers, Omonia is convenient to the Acropolis and other ancient sights just to the south, to the National Archaeological Museum to the north, and to Psyrri, the city's trendiest nightlife district. Wherever you stay, the city's extensive subway and bus network makes it easy to get just about anywhere you'll want to go.

A plush double room at the King George Palace, which has been home to heads of state and celebrities since 1936.

kids Hotel Tony KOUKAKI   Half the basic but spotless units here have kitchenettes, and guests can also use a communal kitchen or grill on the roof terrace—a boon for families and travelers on a tight budget. The south-of-Acropolis neighborhood is quiet but handy to sights and restaurants. *26 Zacharitsa St. ☎ 210/923-0561 or 210/923-5761. www.hoteltony.gr. 21 units. Doubles 60€. No credit cards. Metro: Syngrou-Fix or trolley: 1, 5, 15. Map p 135.*

★ **Jason Inn** PSYRRI   Don't be put off by the dull streets of the immediate vicinity—at this basic but cheerful and well run hotel you are at the edge of the city's trendy enclaves of Psyrri, Gazi, and Thissio and just steps from the busy Monastiraki cafes. The ancient Kerameikos cemetery, some of the city's most intriguing ruins, are just across the street. *12 Agion Asomaton St. ☎ 210/325-1106. Reservations ☎ 210/520-2491. www.douros-hotels.com. 57 units. Doubles 75€–95€ w/breakfast. MC, V. Metro: Thissio. Map p 136.*

★ **King George Palace** SYN-TAGMA   An Athenian landmark matches the neighboring Grand Bretagne for style and opulence, housing guests in sumptuous rooms full of handcrafted furniture and rich fabrics. Among the many amenities are an indoor pool and sauna and a roof garden with sweeping views of the city. *3 Vas. Georgiou St. ☎ 210/322-2210. www.classicalhotels.com. 78 units. Doubles 320€–740€. Metro: Syntagma. Map p 137.*

★ **Meliá Athens** OMONIA   One of several exciting new hotels in gritty Omonia (see Art Hotel Athens and Fresh Hotel) is almost resortlike, with a stunning rooftop pool and spa and soothing neutral-tone rooms, complete with Jacuzzi tubs in the bathrooms. *28 Octovriou St. ☎ 210/332-0100. www.melia-athens. com. 130 units. Doubles from 90€. AE, DC, MC, V. Metro: Omonia. Map p 136.*

★ **Ochre & Brown** PSYRRI   The Psyrri clubs are just outside the door, but the beautifully designed rooms, excellent in-house bar/restaurant, and relaxed, intimate atmosphere here may tempt you into staying put. *7 Leokoriou St. ☎ 210/331-2950. www.oandbhotel.com. 17 units. Doubles 145€–280€ w/breakfast. AE, MC, V. Metro: Thissio or Monastiraki. Map p 136.*

★ **Periscope** KOLONAKI   The over-the-top decor—all grays and whites and ceilings covered with aerial views of the city—doesn't sacrifice comfort and does justice to the

An old stunner steals the show at the stylish, contemporary O&B (see p 145).

stylish neighborhood. Some of the city's best shopping and cafe life is just outside the door. *22 Haritos St.* ☎ *210/729-7200. www.periscope.gr. 21 units. Doubles 160€ w/breakfast. AE, DC, MC, V. Metro: Syntagma or bus: 022, 060, 200. Map p 137.*

Philippos Hotel MAKRIYANNI You can see the Acropolis from most of the sleekly furnished rooms and balconies, and many rooms are set up for families, with an extra bed or pullout couch. A sunny coffee shop adjoins the lobby. *3 Mitseon St.* ☎ *210/922-3611. www.philippos hotel.gr. 50 units. Doubles 75€– 130€. AE, DC, MC, V. Metro: Akropoli. Map p 135.*

★★ St. George Lycabettus KOLONAKI Large, nicely decorated guest rooms (each floor has a different theme, from art nouveau to minimalism) and a beautiful rooftop pool do justice to a wonderful location—the pine-scented slopes of Mt. Lycabettus just above the designer-boutique-lined streets of Kolonaki. *78 Kleomenous.* ☎ *210/729-0711. www.sglycabettus.gr. 159 units. Doubles 140€–200€. AE, DC, MC, V. Bus: 22, 60, or 200. Map p 137.*

★ Semiramis KIFISSIA This stunning design statement by British-Egyptian architect Karim Rashid glows with different colors at night, announcing what lies within—boldly decorated guest quarters where every piece of furniture is a work of art, sweeping lounges, and a neon-lit bar and restaurant. Surrounding Kifissia is a delightfully old-world enclave of shady lanes, neoclassical mansions, and pleasant cafes. *48 Harialou St.* ☎ *210/623-3521. www. semiramisathens.com. 51 units. Doubles 180€–265€. AE, DC, MC, V. Metro: Kifissia. Map p 136.*

Student & Travellers Inn PLAKA When location matters and budget is an issue, look no farther than this well-run hostel on a pretty pedestrian street at the edge of the Plaka. Accommodations are in multi-bunk dorms or, for those with a bit more cash to burn, in one of the private rooms, some of which have private bathrooms and are set up for families. *16 Kydathineon St.* ☎ *210/ 324-4808. www.hihostels.com. 25 units (61 beds). Doubles from 42€ shared facilities; 70€ private. No credit cards. Metro: Syntagma. Map p 136.* ●

Corinth

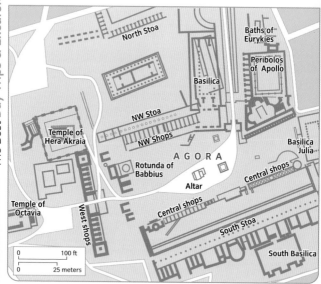

A settlement that began to take shape as early as 5000 B.C., Corinth flourished as one of the most important and wealthiest cities of classical Greece. Corinth fought in the Trojan and Persian Wars and was a major sea power that established a huge colony at Siracusa on the island of Sicily. The Romans destroyed much of Corinth when they overran Greece in the 2nd century B.C., and Julius Caesar ordered the reconstruction of the city in A.D. 52.

① ★★ **Ancient City.** The most imposing ruins of the Greek city are those of the Temple of Apollo, on a low hillock from which 7 of the original 38 Doric columns still rise. Corinth was a major trading center, with sea routes to the Middle East as well as Italy, where the Corinthians established a huge and powerful colony on the island of Sicily. Most of the city that remains was built by the Romans, whose shops line the forum; on the Bema, a raised platform for public speaking that rises amid the forum

ruins, St. Paul went before the Roman prosecutor Gallio in A.D. 52 and pleaded his innocence against accusations that he was persuading the populace to worship God in unlawful ways. The Romans refurbished the Greek Theater, adding rows of seats and engineering the arena so it could be flooded for naval battles. ⏱ *2 hr.*

② ★★★ **Acrocorinth.** The acropolis of ancient Corinth stands sentinel some 540m (1,700 ft.) above the coastal plain and has been a lookout

Previous page: A tholos (round temple) dedicated to Athena is one of many sacred shrines of Delphi.

Practical Matters: Corinth

Corinth is 90km (56 miles) southwest of Athens. If you're driving, you can shoot down to Corinth in an hour or so on the E94 toll road. **KTEL buses** (☎ 210/880-8080 or 210/831-7096 in Athens) leave from Athens Stathmos Leoforia Peloponnisou station (100 Kifissou St.) about every hour and the trip takes 1 to 2 hours, depending on traffic and the number of stops; in Corinth you'll have to a catch a local bus to the ancient site. Many tour operators in Athens offer half-day excursions to Corinth, usually for about 60€. Check with **G.O. Tours,** 31–33 Voulis St. (☎ 210/322-5951; www. gotours.com.gr), or **CHAT tours,** 4 Stadiou St. (☎ 210/322-3137; www.chattours.gr). Admission to the site (☎ 27510/76-585; www. culture.gr) is 6€, including the Acrocorinth; it's open April to October daily 8am to 7:30pm, November to March daily 8am to 5pm.

post, place of refuge, and shrine since the 5th century B.C. Byzantines, Franks, Venetians, and Turks all added to the ancient walls and these three rings of massive fortifications, pierced by gates, ramble across the craggy mountaintop. The ruins of the Temple of Aphrodite stand atop the highest reaches of the peak, and in ancient times the reward for the climb to these heights was the company of 1 of the temple's 1,000 prostitutes. Trekkers who make the 3-hour climb now settle for views that sweep across the sea to the east and west and a broad swath of southern Greece. The less adventurous can make the ascent by car or in one of the taxis that wait at the bottom of the peak. ⏱ *1 hr.*

Seven of 38 original columns still surround Corinth's Temple of Apollo.

Mycenae

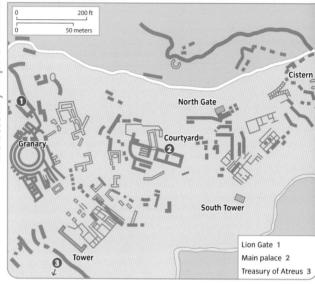

Lion Gate 1
Main palace 2
Treasury of Atreus 3

The short-lived Mycenaean civilization dominated much of the southern Mediterranean from around 1500 B.C. to 1100 B.C. Their greatest city is cradled on a bluff above the fertile Agrolid Plain and surrounded by deep ravines between two barren craggy peaks—a somber setting for this citadel/palace that Homer links with power, riches, and tragedy.

❶ Lion Gate. The fortified entrance to the city is topped by a relief of two lions, now headless, who face each other with their paws resting on a pedestal that supports a column. Holes for the pivots that once supported a massive wooden door sheathed in bronze are still visible, and an adjacent round tower provided a vantage point from which guards could unleash arrows on invaders who breached the gate. A nearby granary was used to store massive quantities of wheat that, with the citadel's water supply delivered by a secret channel, provided insurance against a long siege.

❷ Main palace. Traces of a central hearth and supporting columns are still visible in the throne room of what may have been the palace of King Agamemnon, the Mycenaean king who fought in the Trojan War. Homer, and later the dramatists Aeschylus, Sophocles, and Euripides, wrote about Agamemnon and his doomed clan. Archaeologist Heinrich Schliemann, who rather romantically intertwined myth and historical fact, conjectured that a bathtub in an apartment adjoining the ceremonial hall was the very one in which the king was slain by his adulterous wife, Clytemnestra.

Practical Matters: Mycenae

Mycenae is 115km (71 miles) south of Athens and 50km (30 miles) south of Corinth. If you're driving, you'll probably stop at Corinth first then continue to Mycenae on the toll road, E64, to the Nemea exit, and follow signs from there. **KTEL buses** (☎ 210/880-8080 or 210/831-7096 in Athens) stop about a mile from the site, at Fithia; the bus trip from Athens requires a change in Corinth. Many tour operators in Athens offer one-day excursions to Mycenae and Epidaurus or Mycenae and Corinth. Check with **G.O. Tours,** 31–33 Voulis St. (☎ 210/322-5951; www.gotours.com.gr), or **CHAT tours,** 4 Stadiou St. (☎ 210/322-3137; www.chattours.gr). Admission to the site (☎ 27510/76-585; www.culture.gr) is 8€, including the Treasury of Arteus; it's open April to October daily 8:30am to 7pm, November to March daily 8:30am to 3:30pm.

③ Treasury of Atreus. The largest and grandest Mycenaean tomb consists of a narrow passageway, fashioned out of massive blocks, that leads to a high domed chamber. Already robbed in antiquity, the tomb was the final resting place of royalty. Archaeologist Heinrich Schiliemann found face masks, cups, and jewelry, all fashioned from gold—14 kilos (31 lb.) worth—in several graves at Mycenae during the 1870s; many are now among the holdings of the National Archaeological Museum in Athens (p 38).

The Lion Gate at Mycenae.

Nafplion and Epidaurus

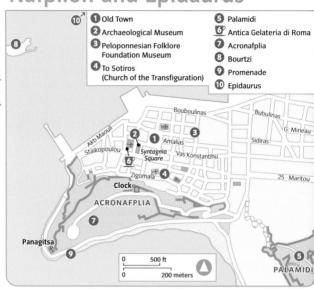

1 Old Town
2 Archaeological Museum
3 Peloponnesian Folklore Foundation Museum
4 To Sotiros (Church of the Transfiguration)
5 Palamidi
6 Antica Gelateria di Roma
7 Acronafplia
8 Bourtzi
9 Promenade
10 Epidaurus

Nafplion is Greece's most beautiful city, built in large part by Byzantines, Franks, Venetians, and Turks who fought over the city, strategically placed on the Gulf of Argos, for centuries. You may well want to combine a visit to Nafplion with a visit to Epidaurus, with its beautifully preserved ancient theater, only half an hour away.

1 ★★★ **Old Town.** Wedged onto a narrow promontory between the sea and the heights dominated by the Acronafplia and Palamidi fortresses, old Nafplion is a delightful place. Tall, proud Venetian town houses line narrow lanes that lead off lovely **Plateia Syntagma** (Constitution Sq.), and two broad, airy seaside promenades, the Bouboulinas and Akti Miaouli, are lined with cafes and patisseries. Palaces, churches, and mosques are remnants of the Venetians and Turks who occupied the city for centuries, and other monuments are from Nafplion's brief tenure as the first capital of Greece, from 1829 to 1834,

when King Otto moved the capital to Athens. ⏱ *2 hr.*

2 ★★ **Archaeological Museum.** A thick-walled Venetian storehouse houses artifacts from the many ancient sites that surround Nafplion. The Mycenaeans steal the show with their splendid craftsmanship, unearthed at Mycenae, Tiryns, Dendra, and other nearby settlements. These include a bronze suit of armor consisting of 15 sheets of bronze so heavy that scholars have concluded the wearer could only have fought while riding in a chariot, and death masks and offerings from the extensive network of tombs at

Mycenae. ⏱ *30 min. Plateia Syntagma.* 📞 *27520/27-502. Admission 2€. Daily 8:30am–3pm.*

③ ★★★ Peloponnesian Folklore Foundation Museum. In this handsome neoclassical house, the emphasis is on beautiful textiles, along with looms and other equipment used to make clothing—harking back to the days when just about all everyday items were made at home. Peloponnesian families donated many of the dowry items and embroidery, though the holdings come from all over Greece and include such rarities as *sperveri*, tents that surround bridal beds in the Dodecanese. Overstuffed drawing rooms from the homes of well-to-do 19th-century Nafpliots provide a glimpse into the comfortable lives of the bourgeoisie. ⏱ *1 hr. Vasileos Alexandrou 1. www.pli.gr. Admission 4€ day, 3€ evening.* 📞 *27520/28-947. Wed–Sat and Mon 9am–3pm and 6–9pm, Sun 9am–3pm.*

④ ★ Tou Sotiros (Church of the Transfiguration). The oldest

Syntagma Square is Nafplion's living room, and its cafes are busy from early morning until well into the night.

church in Nafplion was a convent for Franciscan nuns during the 13th-century Frankish occupation and was refurbished as a mosque by the Turks. A distinctly Christian presence has prevailed since 1839, when Otto, the Bavarian King who

The Bourtzi, on an islet in the Bay of Argos, is one of three Venetian-Ottoman fortresses that once defended Nafplion.

served as monarch of a united Greece, presented the church to Greek Catholics and the so-called Philhellenes, the foreigners who fought alongside Greeks for independence from the Turks. The names of the Philhellenes, among them the British poet and adventurer Lord Byron, are inscribed on the columns. 🕐 *15 min. Zigomala, Old Town. Daily 8am–7pm.*

5 ★★ kids **Palamidi.** The mightiest of the three fortresses that defend Nafplion is Venetian, completed in 1714 and surrounded by massive walls and eight bastions. So secure were the Venetians with these defenses that upon completing the Palamidi they left only 80 soldiers in Nafplion, and the Turks easily seized the fortress just 1 year later. Greek rebels then took the fortress from the Turks during the War of Independence in 1821. Prisoners unfortunate enough to be interred in the Palamidi dungeons over the centuries were found to cut the 999 steps that climb the cliff face from the town below. 🕐 *1 hr. Above Old Town.* ☎ *27520/28-036. Admission 3€. Apr–Oct Mon–Fri 8am–7pm, Sat–Sun 8am–3pm; Nov–Mar daily 8am–3pm.*

6 **Antica Gelateria di Roma.** Traditional gelato, better than most you'd find in Italy, is dispensed along with panini and superb espresso. *Farmakopoulou 3.* ☎ *27520/23-520. Daily 10am–midnight. $.*

7 ★★ kids **Acronafplia.** Fortifications have stood at the southeastern heights of Nafplion for some 5,000 years. Until the Venetians arrived in the 13th century, the entire town lived within the walls, out of harm's way from pirates. Scattered among the pine-scented hilltops are the ruins of several castles and forts, a testament to the Byzantine, Frankish, and Venetian powers who have fought for control of Nafplion and the rest of the Peloponnese. A well-fortified Venetian castle, the Castello del Torrione, is the best-preserved of the fortifications. 🕐 *45 min. Dawn to dusk. Free admission.*

8 ★ kids **Bourtzi.** This picturesque 15th-century island fortress in the harbor has witnessed pirate attacks, served as headquarters for the town executioners, and was once equipped with a massive chain

Nafplion's town beach is tucked onto the shoreline beneath the Acronafplia Fortress.

Practical Matters: Nafplion

Nafplion is 145km (90 miles) southwest of Athens. If you're driving, you can make the drive in less than 2 hours on the E94/E65 toll roads. **KTEL buses** (☎ 210/880-8080 or 210/831-7096 in Athens) leave from Athens Stathmos Leoforia Peloponnisou station (100 Kifissou St.) about every hour and the trip takes 2 to 3 hours, depending on traffic and the number of stops. **G.O. Tours,** 31–33 Voulis St. (☎ 210/322-5951; www.gotours.com.gr) sometimes offers a one-day tour that makes stops in Corinth, Mycenae, Nafplion, and Epidaurus, about 100€ with lunch. You see a lot, but the itinerary doesn't give you much time to enjoy Nafplion.

that the Turks could draw across the harbor to block entry. Boats chug out to the Bourtzoi from the Akti Maouli, the town quay, and from anywhere in town the crenellations and sturdy sexagonal watchtower look like a mirage shimmering across the water. ⏲ *1 hr. for trip out, visit, and return trip. Boat is usually about 5€.*

⑨ ★★★ Promenade. All that remains of the lower walls that were constructed in 1502 to encircle the city is one bastion, the so-called Five Brothers, intended to defend the harbor and named for five Venetian cannons, all bearing the lion of St. Marks. A beautiful seaside promenade beyond the Five Brothers skirts the southeastern tip of the peninsula, following a ledge between the Acronafplia above and the rocky shore below. Arvanitia, at the end of the promenade, is popular with residents who gather here to chat and swim from the rocks and a pebbly beach. ⏲ *1 hr. for walk to Arvanitia and back.*

⑩ ★★★ kids Epidaurus. The Sanctuary of Asklepius at Epidaurus was one of the most famous healing centers in the Greek world. Asklepius, son of Apollo and god of medicine, was worshipped in the beautiful temple at Epidaurus (like much of the sanctuary, undergoing restoration) by cure seekers who were housed in an enormous guesthouse, the Kategogeion. They were treated in the Abaton, where Asklepius came to them in their drug-induced dreams and dispensed advice on cures. The round Tholos appears to have housed the healing serpents that could allegedly cure ailments with a flicker of the tongue over an afflicted body part. The magnificent theater at Epidaurus is one of the best preserved from the ancient world. Buried for close to 1,500 years, the 55 tiers of seats and the stage remain much as they were, and acoustics are so sharp that a stage whisper can be heard at the top of the house. ⏲ *2 hr. Off route 70, outside Ligouria; follow signs to Ancient Theatre.* ☎ *27530/22-009. www. odysseus.culture.gr. Admission, includes theater, sanctuary, and museum, 6€. May–Oct daily 8am– 7pm, Nov–Apr daily 8:30am–3pm.*

Delphi

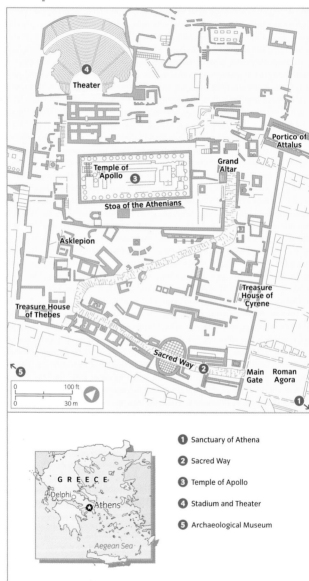

Theater **4**

Portico of Attalus

Temple of Apollo **3**

Grand Altar

Stoa of the Athenians

Asklepion

Treasure House of Cyrene

Treasure House of Thebes

Sacred Way **2**

Main Gate

Roman Agora **1**

5

0 — 100 ft
0 — 30 m

GREECE
Delphi
Athens
Aegean Sea

1 Sanctuary of Athena

2 Sacred Way

3 Temple of Apollo

4 Stadium and Theater

5 Archaeological Museum

No other ancient site is quite as mysterious and alluring as this sanctuary to Apollo, nestled high above the Gulf of Corinth on the flanks of Mount Parnassus. Since it's just 180km/112 miles from central Athens, you can easily visit Delphi in a day. The ruins look their best in the spring, when they are surrounded by wildflowers and the mountain above them is still covered in snow, but are spectacular any time you visit.

1 Sanctuary of Athena.
Slightly below the ancient sight, this terraced sanctuary was the first stop for many pilgrims climbing up the slope from the sea. They would pause to pay homage at such shrines as the exquisitely beautiful and photogenic Tholos (Round) temple, dedicated to an unknown goddess. A shrine has stood on this spot since 1500 B.C., when the Mycenaeans established a sanctuary here to the earth goddess Gaia.

2 Sacred Way. The Temple of Apollo was reached on this monumental walkway, once lined with magnificent temples that city-states erected as votive dedications to Apollo—and as a bit of one-upmanship to see who could outdo one another. These were some of the greatest works of antiquity, filled with treasures. Only foundations remain of all but the Athenian Treasury, restored in the 1930s.

3 Temple of Apollo. It was here, allegedly, that questions inscribed on stone tablets would be presented to a Pythian priestess who had undergone a cleansing and purification ritual. Speaking for Apollo, she would utter garbled verse to priests, who interpreted them and passed along enigmatic statements (setting a precedent adapted by today's politicians). Among the supplicants were rulers and generals who came from throughout the Mediterranean world seeking advice. A famously enigmatic piece of advice was given to King Croesus of Lydia, who asked if he should attack the Persians. If he did so, he was told, he would destroy a great empire—he did attack and he did destroy a kingdom, his own.

4 The Stadium and Theater.
The 4th-century-B.C. theater and nearby stadium hosted the musicians, performers, and athletes who came to Delphi for the Pythian Games, held every 4 years in honor of Apollo. Both afford magnificent views over the sanctuary and surrounding mountains.

5 ★★★ Archaeological Museum. These spacious, well lit galleries show off treasures from the Delphi temples and shrines. Seeing these magnificent works helps bring the importance of the sanctuary to light; time permitting, walk around the site here, then tour the museum to see the ruins one housed, then do

Tholos at Delphi.

Practical Matters: Delphi

Getting to Delphi is relatively easy, as there are usually a few buses daily from the Athens regional Bus Terminal B at 260 Liossion St. (Once in Delphi, you should do all your exploring on foot.) **KTEL buses** (☎ 210/880-8080 or 210/831-7096 in Athens; 226/508-2317 in Delphi) leave six times a day from Athens and take about 3 hours each way. Tickets are 13€. Scores of tour operators in Athens offer 1-day excursions to Delphi. Some tried-and-true operators are **G.O. Tours,** 31–33 Voulis St. (☎ 210/322-5951; www.gotours.com.gr), or **CHAT tours,** 4 Stadiou St. (☎ 210/322-3137); both offer 1- and 2-day trips that leave Athens by 8am and arrive at Delphi by 3pm. One-day tours are about 90€; if you want a little more to enjoy the site, take the 2-day tour—about 150€ including transportation, all admission fees, a guide, hotel, and most meals. If you're traveling on your own, admission to the site (☎ 226/508-2312; www.culture. gr; open May–Oct Tues–Sun 7:30am–7:15pm, Mon noon–6:30pm; Nov–Apr and some holidays 8:30am–3pm) is 6€ or 9€ for the museum and site. For more information on the site or modern town, go to the Delphi town hall tourism office, 12 Frederikis and 11 Apollonos sts. (☎ 226/508-2900), from 7:30am to 2:30pm.

another round of the site using your imagination to put these treasures in place. A bronze statue of a charioteer, one of the great works to come down from ancient Greece, honors a victory during Delphi's Pythian games and is one of the museum's greatest treasures. He is believed to have stood next to the Temple of Apollo. Some of the most fascinating finds are friezes depicting the feats of the gods, the superheroes of the ancient world. A 4th century B.C. marble egg *(omphalos)*, a reproduction of an even older version, honors Delphi's position as the center of the ancient world. Legend has it that Zeus released two eagles from Mount Olympus to fly around the world in opposite directions; where they met would be the center of the world and that, of course, was Delphi. ●

Delphi is nestled in rugged mountains at what ancients believed was the center of the world.

The
Savvy Traveler

Before You Go

Government Tourist Offices

In the U.S.: Greek National Tourism Organization (GNTO), Olympic Tower, 645 Fifth Ave., Ste. 903, New York, NY 10022 (☎ 212/421-5777; fax 212/826-6940; www.greek tourism.com). **In Canada:** Hellenic Tourism Organization, 1500 Don Mills Rd., Ste. 102, Toronto, Ontario M3B-3K4 (☎ 416/968-2220; fax 416/968-6533). **In the U.K. and Ireland:** GNTO, 4 Conduit St., London W1S 2DJ (☎ 020/7495-9300; fax 020/7495-4057; www.gnto. co.uk). **In Australia and New Zealand:** GNTO, 37–49 Pitt St., Sydney, New South Wales 2000 (☎ 02/9241-1663; fax 02/9241-2499). **In Greece:** GNTO, 7 Tsoha St., Ambelokipi, Athens 11521 (☎ 210/870-7000; www. gnto.gr); 26 Amalias Ave., Syntagma, Athens 10557 (☎ 210/331-0392; fax 210/331-0640; www.gnto.gr).

The Best Times to Go

Athens temperatures are most comfortable in the **fall** and full-bloom **spring,** when it is also at its most beautiful. It is hottest in June and July, but this is also the time when **summer** festivals are in full swing. The northern *Meltemia* (Etesian winds) blow from mid-July to mid-August, when chilly Aegean Sea water is warmest. Except for tourist areas like Plaka, this city of four million empties during the August 15 national holiday week, when most Greeks go on holiday. Athens—and budget hotels without heat—can get very chilly from November to March.

Festivals & Special Events

SPRING   The Greek calendar revolves around religious holidays, and **Orthodox Easter** (*Pascha*), usually a week later than Western Easter, is the nation's biggest. Many Athenians fast during Holy Week. Church bells toll on Good Friday, and candlelight processions wind through neighborhoods. On Saturday night, the faithful go to their neighborhood churches just before midnight with candles to celebrate Resurrection (*Anastasi*). The priest brings out the holy flame and passes it to the congregation, who light candles while saying "*Christos anesti*" (Christ is risen). Youths light fireworks, and congregants bless their homes by "drawing" a cross on the door frame with smoke from the candles they've brought from church. The Lenten fast is broken by cracking red-dyed eggs and eating soup made with lamb innards. Lamb is spit-roasted on Sunday on rooftops, in garages, in backyards, and in parks. Easter Monday is a national holiday.

SUMMER   **Music, art, and film festivals** kick off in May and June (see p 128). Athens is deserted in August, especially around August 15 (for the **Assumption of the Virgin** holiday).

FALL   Athens hosts an **International Film Festival** (www.aiff.gr) in September. Fashionistas arrive for **Fashion Week** (www.hfda.gr) at Zappeion Gardens in October, and the **Marathon** (☎ 210/933-1113; www.athensclassicmarathon.gr), from namesake Marathon to Athens, takes place in November.

WINTER   City streets and squares are decked out in December and January for **Christmas** and **New Year's** festivities. Syntagma Square is enlivened with the biggest Christmas tree in town, a carousel, and lots of street stalls. New Year's celebrants gather in Syntagma or in Kotzia Square in front of City Hall. Men

Previous page: The Metro passing under the illuminated Hephaisteion temple in the Ancient

ATHENS'S AVERAGE TEMPERATURES & PRECIPITATION					
	JAN	FEB	MAR	APR	MAY	JUNE
TEMP (°F)	49	50	53	60	68	76
TEMP (°C)	9	10	12	16	20	24
RAINFALL (IN.)	1.80	1.90	1.70	1.10	0.70	0.40
RAINFALL (CM)	4.57	4.83	4.32	2.79	1.78	1.02
	JULY	AUG	SEPT	OCT	NOV	DEC
TEMP (°F)	81	80	74	65	58	52
TEMP (°C)	27	27	23	18	14	11
RAINFALL (IN.)	0.20	0.20	0.50	1.90	2.00	2.60
RAINFALL (CM)	0.51	0.51	1.27	4.83	5.08	6.60

dive into frigid waters at the port of Piraeus to retrieve the cross on **Epiphany** (Jan 6). February's pre-Lent **Carnival** (*Karnavali* or *Apokries*) is celebrated with costume parades and merriment—people bop each other with plastic bats in the Plaka. When Lent begins on **Clean Monday** in February or March, Athenians picnic and fly kites on Filopappou Hill. Military parades are seen on **Independence Day,** March 25.

The Weather
Basically there are two seasons, borne out by the traditional weather-change send-offs "*Kalo Himona*" (Good Winter) or "*Kalo Kalokairi*" (Good Summer). Summer, generally starting after Easter, is very hot and dry, often reaching 40°C (104°F). As the saying goes, only mad dogs and Englishmen would venture out in the midday sun, hence the siesta between 3 and 6pm. The seasonal north (Etesian) winds blow mid-July to mid-August, but it can get very windy anytime, stopping ferry transport. Torrential rains can also occur quickly.

Winter is mild and rainy and light snow is not unheard of. Many buildings are not insulated, and the centrally controlled heating is often intermittent, making the cold season very long indeed.

Useful Websites
- **www.culture.gr:** The culture ministry of Greece's web page for museums and sites.
- **www.gnto.gr:** The Greece tourism ministry's site.
- **www.ticketnet.gr:** See what Arts & Entertainment events are in town.
- **www.hnms.gr:** The Hellenic National Meteorological Service (weather reports).
- **www.oasa.gr:** A public transportation site, including maps.
- **www.poseidon.ncmr.gr:** The Hellenic Centre for Marine Research's weather site, including sea-surface temperature.
- **www.gntp.gr:** The pages of a private travel organization include detailed ferry schedules.

Cell (Mobile) Phones
As in all of Europe, **GSM (Global System for Mobiles)** phones work in Greece, but making and receiving calls can be expensive. It is probably cheaper to buy a phone to use while in Athens. **Kapa Change,** at 52 Mitropoleos St. (☎ 210/331-0493; www.kapatravel.gr), sells mobiles from 25€ and a Greek phone number from 1€.

Getting **There**

By Plane

Eleftherios Venizelos, the Athens International Airport (☎ 210/353-0000; www.aia.gr) in Spata (27km/17 miles east of Athens), is a major south-European hub. There are two airport information desks at each end of the arrivals hall, three ATMs, two free Internet kiosks, a pharmacy, a post office, a money exchange machine manned at the departure level, and a few shops. The **Greek National Tourism Organization** (GNTO or EOT in Greek; ☎ 210/353-0445) is also in the arrivals hall, alongside private tour agencies that can book hotels.

Getting into Town from the Airport

The **Metro** subway (☎ 210/519-4012; www.ametro.gr) goes to central Athens (45 min.) from the airport, or you can take the suburban railway **Proastiakos** (☎ 210/527-2000; www.oasa.gr; www.proastiakos.gr) to Larissa Station, Athens's central railway station (40 min.), to the port of Piraeus (1 hr.), or to Corinth (1½ hr.). Tickets for either the Metro or Proastiakos are 6€ (3€ for children 17 and under or adults 65 and over; free for children 5 and under; 10€ for two people; 15€ for three people), which you validate or "cancel" in machines before you get to the shared platform. Don't forget—fines up to 60 times the fare are levied if you don't cancel and get caught. Metro and Proastiakos services run from about 7am to 11pm.

Public buses (☎ 185; www.oasa.gr) terminate outside the arrivals hall, and tickets, which you validate on machines on the bus, cost 3.20€. Both the X94 and X95 run to the Ethniki Amyna Metro station on Line Three if you want to take the rest of your journey into town on the Metro from there. X95 continues to central Syntagma Square, about a 70-minute trip. Bus X96 stops at the Faliro Metro station (which connects with the **tram**) before continuing on to the port of Piraeus Metro station; both of those stops are also on Metro Line One.

A **taxi** will cost around 30€, and around 40€ between midnight and 5am. Trip time is 30 minutes to an hour, depending on traffic. There are additional charges, such as for luggage, tolls, and time, which do not appear on the meter. The charges are usually listed on a card mounted on the dashboard, where the driver's ID should also be mounted.

By Ferry

Boats from Ancona, Bari, Brindisi, and Venice, Italy, arrive daily to the ports of Patras and Igoumenitsa. Trip times vary depending on the ferry you take and your departure and arrival points, but it takes from 10 to 17 hours to get to the main arrival port of Patras. Eurailpass holders should consult **www.raileurope.com** or their pass booklets to see which operators will honor their passes. Note that you'll have to pay a port tax, fuel fees, and a seasonal surcharge (16€–26€) even if you do have a pass. When you factor in the cost of food and possibly a berth, you'll probably discover it's cheaper to fly.

Trains from the port at Patras (☎ 1110 or 26106/39-102) to Athens take 3½ hours and cost 5.30€, while a long-distance **KTEL bus** (☎ 21051/47-310 in Athens; 26106/23-887 in Patras) that leaves every 30 to 45 minutes takes 2½ hours and costs about 15€.

By Cruise Ship

Cruise ship passengers can get from the port of Piraeus into Athens (10km/6 miles/20 min.) by taking bus no. 049 at the terminus on main Akti Miaouli Avenue, near the international passenger terminal, to the terminus on Athinas Street in Athens. You can also walk around the harbor (15–20 min.) to the Piraeus Metro station (20 min. to Athens) or hail a cab (15–30 min. to Athens; about 10€).

By Train

Greece is connected to the Balkans, Eastern Europe, Russia, and Turkey by a rather lurching rail system, with international trains terminating in the northern port city of Thessaloniki. Check the English page of the German website **Die Bahn** (http://reiseauskunft.bahn.de) for international journeys, and the **Hellenic National Railway** (OSE; ☎ 1110; www.ose.gr) for domestic travel. You can reserve up to a month in advance, but you must buy your ticket at a domestic station or OSE-affiliated travel agency not less than 48 hours before your journey. The two OSE ticket offices in Athens are at 1 Karolou St. (☎ 1110), open Monday to Friday 8am to 3pm, and at 6 Sina St. (international travel: ☎ 210/362-7947; domestic travel: ☎ 1110; from abroad: ☎ 210/362-1039), open Monday to Saturday 8am to 3:30pm.

There are some 11 trains daily from Thessaloniki to Athens's relatively small Larissa OSE Station (☎ 210/529-8829), and the trip

takes from 4½ to 8 hours for overnights, which have sleepers that range from 54€ in a single compartment to 24€ in a six-bed. Larissa Station has luggage storage, a restaurant, a platform cantina, and a train information counter. Only same-day tickets can be purchased in the building's main entrance. Advance tickets are available from the south end (outside the entrance) toward the kiosk.

By Bus

The KTEL regional **Bus Terminal A** (with buses to Patras, points north and south, Peloponnese, and western Greece) is at 100 Kifissou St. (☎ 210/512-4910). The local bus 051 from Menandrou Street, west of Omonia Square in Athens, gets you there. **Bus Terminal B** (to central Greece, including Delphi and Meteora) is at 260 Liossion St. (☎ 210/831-7153), and is served by a dozen city buses that go to Attiki Metro station. The driver usually drops passengers off near Kato Patissia station on Line One, however, before reaching the terminal. Buses to sites in Attica (including Cape Sounion and Marathon) leave from **Aigyptou Square** on Patission Street (☎ 210/822-5148, 210/880-8080; www.ktelattikis.gr), just past the National Archaeological Museum. Buses going abroad, to Turkey and Albania for example, are run by KTEL (☎ 1421; www.ktel.org), the Hellenic National Railway (see "By Train" above), and private travel agencies.

Getting **Around**

By Bus

Local buses and trolleys run from about 5am to 10pm, occasionally to midnight, depending on the line. Tickets are 1€ and are bought in

advance from *periptera* (kiosks) or at bus-ticket booths at some bus stops. Families with four or more children are entitled to reduced fare. Tickets are valid for 90 minutes on all modes of public transport and must be validated (or "canceled") in the machine upon boarding. **Athens Urban Transport Organization** (OASA; ☎ 185; www.oasa.gr) puts out a route map, and you can check it online. There is a state-run hop-on sightseeing bus that does a circuit of all the main sites in 80 to 90 minutes. The 6€ ticket can be purchased on the bus (no. 400), which is good for 24 hours on all public transport within the city.

By Metro

Tickets for the three lines—**green Line One** (run by ISAP), the **red Line Two,** and the **blue Line Three**—are 1€. You may use them for travel on all three lines and all modes of public transport for 90 minutes.

A 3€ ticket buys you 24 hours; a 10€ ticket is valid for 7 days. These can be purchased at bus-ticket booths, kiosks, and tram, Metro, and Proastiakos stations. See the **Metro** (www.ametro.gr) and **OASA** (www.oasa.gr) websites for more options.

By Tram

The **tram** (www.tramsa.gr) goes from Syntagma Square to the coast, where it branches west to the Neo Faliro district and nearby Peace and Friendship stadium, and southeast past beaches at Alimos and Hellenikon to Glyfada and Voula.

Tram tickets, purchased at station vending machines or at manned ticket booths at some stations, cost 1€ and are valid on all modes of public transport within 90 minutes of validation. The tram runs from 5am to midnight.

By Taxi

Rates, normally posted on the dashboard, start at 1€ and the minimum fare is 2.80€. The meter rate of .50€ per kilometer nearly doubles if you leave the city limits (not including the airport) or for travel between midnight and 5am. Other charges can be added for airport, port, and bus station pickups and drop-offs, heavy luggage, tolls, and waiting time.

Taxis can pick up other passengers going to destinations on the route, a practice that helps keep the rates down.

Taxis can be difficult to find around 3pm (the shift change) and 11:30pm (when they all wait till the night tariff kicks in). There are some 15 taxi companies in Athens that you can call to make an appointment for immediate service—and pay 2€ to 5€ extra for the privilege. Two are **Attika** (☎ 210/341-0553) and **Ikaros** (☎ 210/515-2800). Or call **Limotours,** 20 Syngrou Ave. (☎ 210/922-0333; www.limotours. gr); **Athens Luxury Transportation Services** (☎ 210/322-4587; www.athensexclusivetaxi.gr); or **George the Famous Taxi Driver** (☎ 210/963-7030; georgetaxitours@ yahoo.com) for trips to the airport, tours, and so on.

By Car

Driving in central Athens is not recommended. Traffic is heavy, most streets are one-way or pedestrian, parking is difficult and expensive, and drivers use the meter can be erratic. The historic center is fairly compact so there is really no need to drive. Many car-rental offices are located at the top of Syngrou Avenue in Makriyanni.

By Foot

You can reach most of the main sites in Athens on foot or on the Metro. Much of the historic and commercial center is pedestrianized, including touristy Plaka, and a walkway—the Grand Promenade—links up Hadrian's Arch, the Parthenon, Filopappou Hill, the Ancient Agora and Thissio, Monastiraki Square, the Roman Agora, and the ancient Kerameikos cemetery and Technopolis cultural center in Gazi.

Wear comfortable shoes and watch your step—a lot of sidewalks are blocked (by cars, motorcycles, or trees), slippery (paved with marble), soiled (Athenians like dogs), or uneven. Drivers rarely yield right of way to pedestrians, so don't blindly step into the road even if the light is green. Always look both ways before crossing the street.

Fast **Facts**

APARTMENT RENTALS Check long-term rates of apartment hotels in the Lodging chapter, the classifieds in the weekly **Athens News** (www. athensnews.gr), or online sites such as **www.vacationhomerentals. com** or **http://athens.craigslist.gr**.

AREA CODES The country code for Greece is **30**. Domestically, 10 digits are needed, which includes the area code. Athens's numbers take 210 or 211 plus seven digits; Thessaloniki takes an area code (2310) plus six digits, as does Patras (2610) and other urban areas. A five-digit area code is used elsewhere in the country. Mobile (cell) phones do not follow the area-code rule but require 10 digits and begin with 6.

ATMS & CASH POINTS ATMs are widely available—Greece has a lot of banks. Both your bank and the Greek bank will charge you for the transaction.

BABYSITTING Hotels can often arrange babysitting.

BANKING HOURS Generally, banks are open Monday to Thursday 8am to 2:30pm and Friday 8am to 2pm.

BIKE RENTALS For tours and rentals, try **Pame Volta** (☎ 210/675-2886; www.pamevolta.gr).

BUSINESS HOURS Work hours in Greece differ by season, day of the week, and type of business. Shops are generally open Monday, Wednesday, and Saturday from 8:30am to 2pm; Tuesday, Thursday, and Friday from 8:30am to 2pm and again from 5:30 to 8:30pm. Chain stores, supermarkets, and department stores remain open through the midday siesta Monday through Saturday. In tourist areas, stores are generally open longer, as well as on Sundays.

CONSULATES & EMBASSIES **U.S. Embassy:** 91 Vas. Sofias Ave. (☎ 210/721-2951; www.usembassy. gr); Metro: Megaron Mousikis. **Canadian Embassy:** 4 Ioannou Gennadiou St. (☎ 210/727-3400; www.athens.gc.ca); Metro: Evangelismos. **U.K. Embassy:** 1 Ploutarchou St. (☎ 210/727-2600; www. british-embassy.gr); Metro: Evangelismos. **Australian Embassy:** Thon Building, Kifissias and Alexandras aves. (☎/fax 210/870-4000; www. greece.embassy.gov.au); Metro: Ambelokipi. **New Zealand Consulate:** 76 Kifissias Ave. (☎ 210/692-4136); Metro: Ambelokipi. **Irish Embassy:** 7 Vas. Konstantinou St., opposite Panathenian Stadium (☎ 210/732-2771), Metro: Acropolis.

CRIME & SAFETY Young women may get propositioned by shopkeepers in tourist areas and the unsuspecting may be scammed but not harmed. Greece has a low crime rate and you can safely walk the streets well into the night, but pickpocketing, mostly on public transport during busy times, is a problem. Motorcycle thieves may also target the vulnerable by pulling up alongside and grabbing shoulder bags, pulling you over in the process.

Walk against the traffic to avoid motorcycle-riding purse snatchers. Don't accept offers of possibly drugged food or water from strangers at tourist sites, and avoid touts that take lone males to hostess bars or hotel-room parties. You will pay exorbitant bills if you succumb. Taxi drivers are notorious for overcharging, or giving you change for a smaller denomination bill. Put your hand over the keypad at ATMs when you enter your PIN to avoid card theft.

CUSTOMS You may bring a total of 175€ worth of gift items into Greece, as well as: 200 cigarettes, 1 liter of alcohol or 2 liters of wine, and 22 pounds of food and beverages.

DINING For breakfast and snacks, countless holes-in-the-wall sell various pies, *tiropita* (cheese), *spanakopita* (spinach), and *bougatsa* (cream/semolina). *Koulouri* (round bread "sticks") are sold in the street, as are roasted chestnuts and corn on the cob. The midday meal, eaten at around 2 or 3pm, is the biggest. Dinner hour is 10pm.

DOCTORS & DENTISTS See "Emergencies" and "Hospitals."

ELECTRICITY Electric current in Greece is 220 volts AC, alternating at 50 cycles. Appliances from North America that are not dual voltage will require a transformer and a round two-prong adapter plug.

EMERGENCIES For emergencies throughout Greece, dial ☎ **100** for police assistance or ☎ **171** for the Tourist Police. Dial ☎ **199** to report a fire and ☎ **166** for an ambulance. The E.U.-wide ☎ **112** is a multilingual service for all kinds of emergencies.

If you need an English-speaking doctor or dentist, call your embassy for advice or the 24-hour **SOS Doctors** (☎ **1016**; www.sosiatroi.gr). Some American- and British-trained doctors and hospitals offering

emergency services advertise in the English-language *Athens News*, available at kiosks that sell international press. Most of the larger hotels have doctors whom they can call for you in an emergency.

Major hospitals rotate emergency duty daily; call ☎ **1434** to hear recorded information in Greek on whose turn it is, or ☎ **112** for the multilingual European Union emergency hotline, or consult the English edition of the *Kathimerini* daily newspaper, distributed with the *International Herald Tribune,* sold wherever you see the foreign press and online at **www.ekathimerini.com**.

EVENT LISTINGS The most complete listings for arts or entertainment are in Greek only. Try the weekly *Athinorama* or *Time Out* and ask your hotel or at tourist information for assistance; many hotels distribute English-language publications geared to entertainment and dining. There are limited listings in the weekly *Athens News* or daily *Kathimerini* section inside the *International Herald Tribune.* For festivals and happenings in Athens, see **www.dolphin-hellas.gr**, and click on Cultural Events.

FAMILY TRAVEL Expect preferential treatment. Ask your hotel for special needs such as cots, bottle warming, and connecting rooms. Most restaurants welcome children, but check stroller access; the same goes for museums and sites. Children 5 and under ride free on public transport; children 17 and under and seniors get 50% off the Metro and Proastiakos rail; and families with four or more children are eligible for reduced fares on buses.

GAY & LESBIAN TRAVELERS Check **www.gaygreece.gr** or **www.10percent.gr**. The Gazi area has many gay-friendly bars and clubs.

HEALTH Sunglasses, sunscreen, and a hat are necessities in summer. Keep in the shade as much as possible, and carry water with you. Tap water in Athens is safe to drink and quite pleasant tasting, and bottled water is widely available in corner stores, kiosks, and other shops. Embassies and some hotels can provide info on English-speaking doctors if you fall ill. State hospitals treat minor emergencies free of charge; otherwise, admission is possible through a doctor.

HOLIDAYS Greece celebrates New Year's Day (Jan 1); Epiphany (Jan 6); Clean (Ash) Monday (Feb or Mar); Independence Day (Mar 25); Good Friday and Easter Sunday and Monday (in the Orthodox calendar, Apr or May); Labor Day (May 1); Whit Monday (May or June); the Assumption of the Virgin (Aug 15); Ochi Day (Oct 28); Christmas and the day after (Dec 25–26); and the student uprising commemoration march to the U.S. Embassy (Nov 17).

HOSPITALS There is a walk-in **first-aid clinic** on the corner of Panagi Tsaldari and Socratous streets, near Omonia Square (1 block up from Geraniou St.). One private hospital is **Euroclinic** (☎ 210/641-6600; www.euroclinic.gr), at 9 Athanasiadou St. (off Soutsou St.); Metro: Ambelokipi.

INSURANCE Check if you're covered already from medical, home, work, or travel policies in your home country. You can try for the best deal through "supermarket" websites such as **www.moneysupermarket.com/travelinsurance**. E.U. residents are covered with the **European Health Insurance Card** (EHIC; www.ehic.org.uk).

INTERNET ACCESS You'll find many Internet cafes in Athens, including the centrally located **Plaka Internet World**, 29 Pandrossou St. (☎ 210/331-6056; Metro: Monastaraki). You can view a list of cybercafes in Athens at www.athensinfoguide.com/geninternet.htm. Many bars and other businesses are equipped with Wi-Fi for patrons, and all of Syntagma Square is a Wi-Fi hot zone. Most hotels are also Wi-Fi equipped; ironically, more expensive hotels often charge quite a bit to utilize Wi-Fi connections while the service is often free at less expensive hotels. Many hotels also have a computer with an Internet connection that guests can use for free or a small fee.

LAUNDRY Many hotels offer laundry services; while laundering can be quite costly in more expensive hotels, many less expensive hotels offer these services at extremely reasonable rates and some have self-serve laundry facilities. A centrally located laundromat is National, in the Plaka at 17 Apollonos St. (☎ 210/323-2226; Metro: Syntagma). It's open Monday and Wednesday from 7am to 4pm and Tuesday, Thursday, and Friday from 7am to 8pm.

LOST PROPERTY File a report at the nearest police station. On trains call ☎ **1110;** on the Metro call ☎ **210/327-9630** or go to Syntagma station.

MAIL & POSTAGE Overseas postcard stamps cost .70€ and are available at many kiosks and shops selling postcards. The main post office is at Syntagma Square at Mitropoleos Street; another is at 100 Aeolou St., just southeast of Omonia Square. The parcel post office is at 60 Mitropoleos St. Hours are Monday to Friday 7:30am to 8pm. The Aeolou and Syntagma branches are open Saturday 7:30am to 2pm, and Syntagma is also open on Sunday 9am to 1:30pm. Regular post offices are open Monday to Friday 7:30am to 2pm.

MONEY Greece's currency is the euro. In this cash-driven society, most nonchain stores and restaurants do not accept credit or debit cards; try to have bills in small denominations. Apart from ATM withdrawals, you can get money wired through **Money Gram** agents (www.moneygram.com) and **Western Union** (☎ 801/113-8000), which are located at post offices and exchange bureaus, such as at Syntagma Square and at 52 Mitropoleos St. There's an **American Express** bank at 43 Akademias St. (☎ 210/363-5960).

NEWSPAPERS & MAGAZINES English-language newspapers are found at foreign-press newsstands, including all the kiosks at the top of Ermou Street at Syntagma Square. A foreign-press kiosk at Omonia Square is open 24 hours (see p 67). The **Athens News** (www.athensnews.gr) is a weekly English-language newspaper, and **Kathimerini** (www.ekathimerini.com) is a daily found inside the *International Herald Tribune*.

PARKING Parking is difficult. You can take your chances and park on streets where you see other cars (the signs are confusing), but it's best to use your hotel parking service or a parking garage. Charges are about 5€ for the first hour and 16€ a day.

PASSES A 12€ ticket to the **Acropolis**—a coupon booklet—is valid for 4 days, and includes admission coupons to the Acropolis, Acropolis Museum, Ancient Agora, Theater of Dionysos and south slope, Tower of the Winds, Kerameikos Cemetery, Roman Forum, north slope, and the Temple of Olympian Zeus.

Eurailpass holders should check their booklets for discounts on hotels, tours, and domestic ferry journeys.

PASSPORTS Most foreigners, including North Americans who stay less than 3 months, do not need a visa, just a valid passport. A

passport usually is required when registering in a hotel and kept until checkout.

PHARMACIES Pharmacies are marked by green and sometimes red crosses, and are usually open from 8 or 10am to 2pm and again from 5 to 8:30pm on Tuesday, Thursday, and Friday. After-hours locations are posted (in Greek) in pharmacy windows, found by dialing ☎ 1434 (in Greek), or by looking in an **Athens News** or **Kathimerini** newspaper or on **www.ekathimerini.com**. You can get antibiotics and other over-the-counter meds without a prescription, along with advice for simple ailments.

POLICE Dial ☎ 100. For help dealing with a troublesome taxi driver or hotel, restaurant, or shop owner, call the **Tourist Police** at ☎ 171; they're on call 24 hours and speak English, as well as other foreign languages.

SENIOR TRAVELERS Seniors (60 or 65 and over) pay less at most museums and sites, on the Metro and Proastiakos suburban railway (65 and over), and at organized beaches (65 and over). Always ask if discounts are available. **Elderhostel** (www.elderhostel.org) does tours. For accessibility issues, see "Travelers with Disabilities," below.

SMOKING Smoking is allowed almost anywhere, but even Athenians are smoking less and becoming a bit less tolerant of those who do smoke.

STUDENT TRAVEL Athens has long been a popular stopover for student travelers and continues to offer the appeal of being less expensive than many European cities. A student ID will usually gain you admission to museums and sites at reduced rates; the most widely accepted form of student identification is an International Student Identity Card

(ISIC), available from STA Travel (☎ 800/781-4040; www.sta.com). Membership in Hosteling International-American Youth Hostels will gain you access to the city's youth hostels, but you'll probably be able to find comparable rates at some hotels (see chapter 9); for more information and a list of hostels in Athens, go to www.hiayh.org.

TELEPHONES Most public phones accept only phone cards, which are available at kiosks. **Telecards** come in denominations from 3€ to 18€. Local calls cost .05€ per minute. International rates vary, with calls to the U.S., Canada, and Australia (Zone I) costing .30€ per minute. **Prepaid calling cards** are available at kiosks, post offices, OTEshop (phone company) outlets, and money-exchange bureaus (which can also tell you what card gives the best rate for the country you want to call). Denominations are usually 5€, 10€, and 20€. Other phone companies include **AT&T** (☎ 00/800-1311); **MCI** (☎ 00/800-1211); and **Sprint** (☎ 00/800-1411). For international phone assistance, dial ☎ **139.**

TAXES A value-added tax (VAT), normally 19%, is included in the price of goods, less for items like books and food. Keep your receipts and go to **Eurochange** in the airport's departure hall.

TIME ZONE Athens and the rest of Greece is 2 hours ahead of Greenwich Mean Time. This means Athens is 2 hours ahead of London, 7 hours ahead of New York, and 10 hours ahead of San Francisco. Greece observes Daylight Saving Time, though often the time changes on a schedule different from that observed in North America.

TIPPING Round up to the nearest euro in a taxi; leave 10% to 20% at restaurants and bars. Restaurants include a service charge in the bill, but many add a 10% tip. Hotel chambermaids should get at least 1€ per day and bellhops 1€ to 2€, depending on the service.

TOILETS Metro stations do not have toilets, but coin-operated facilities are often located nearby. Some squares have public toilets, but most people use the facilities at restaurants and cafes.

TOURIST OFFICES The **Greek National Tourism Organization (GNTO)** head office is at 7 Tsochas St. (☎ 210/870-7000; www.gnto. gr); the central information desk is at 26 Amalias St. (☎ 210/331-0392). A helpful branch (☎ 210/353-0445) is located in the airport's arrivals hall.

Two good online resources are the privately maintained **www. greecetravel.com** and, for sites of interest, the Hellenic Ministry of Culture's **www.culture.gr**.

The **Tourist Police,** 43 Veikou St. (☎ 171 or 210/920-0724), south of the Acropolis, offer round-the-clock tourist information in English.

TRAVELERS WITH DISABILITIES Athens has a fledgling accessibility consciousness. The **European Network for Accessible Tourism** (☎ 210/614-8380; www.accessible tourism.org) has information, or check the relevant transport and hotel websites for accessibility. See **www.europeforall.com** or **www. sath.org** for further information on accessible travel in Greece. The **Tactile Museum for the Blind,** by appointment only, is at 198 Doiranis St. (☎ 210/941-5222).

Athens: **A Brief History**

4500–4000 B.C. The area around Acropolis hill is first settled.

510 B.C. Spartans invade Athens.

508–507 B.C. First Athenian democracy established.

490–480 B.C. Persians defeated at battle of Marathon; fleet defeated at Salamis.

478 B.C. Athens League rule over Greek cities formed.

447–438 B.C. Parthenon built during "Golden Age of Greece."

322 B.C. Macedonian occupation of Athens.

58 B.C. Athens under Roman domination.

A.D. 50 Apostle Paul preaches at Areopagus.

267 Black Sea region Heruls (Goths) raze Athens.

4TH–5TH C. Athens thrives as a major philosophical and education center; Hadrian's Library rebuilt.

529 Justinian I closes the Academy.

582 Slavs and Avars sack the city.

12TH–15TH C. Athens conquered by Franks, Catalans, Venetians, and Ottomans.

1687–1688 Venetian bomb hits Parthenon; Venetian rule.

17TH–18TH C. Ottoman rule.

1801–1803 Britain's Lord Elgin removes metope sculptures from the Parthenon and ships them to England; widespread pillaging of antiquities, especially by England and France.

1821–1830 Greek War of Independence.

1834 Capital moved from Nafplion to Athens.

1843 Constitution demanded from installed Bavarian King Otto in front of the palace, now Parliament, at Syntagma (Constitution) Square.

1896 First modern Olympic Games.

1922–1923 Greece receives 1.1 million refugees from Asia Minor (Turkey); Athens's population doubles between 1920 and 1928.

1940–1941 Italy and then Germany invade and occupy Greece in World War II.

1944 Churchill and Stalin agree on respective spheres of influence over Greece and Romania.

1946–1949 Cold War hostilities fuel civil war.

1956 First general election in which women vote.

1967 Junior disgruntled officers, "the colonels," proclaim martial law, auguring in a brutal 7-year dictatorship.

NOV 17, 1973 Tanks invade Polytechnic campus during student protests; at least 34 killed.

1974 Junta collapses after failed coup in Cyprus; Turkey invades the island. Monarchy abolished in referendum.

1981 Greece becomes 10th member of EEC (European Economic Community).

1991 Greece clashes with newly independent Former Yugoslav Republic of Macedonia (FYROM) over name.

JAN 1996 Greece and Turkey come to brink of war over islet of Imia.

1999 Relations thaw with mutual assistance after earthquakes strike Turkey and Greece.

FEB 3–5, 2000 Turkish Foreign Minister Ismail Cem makes first official visit in 40 years.

SEPT 2000 *Express Samina* sinks near Paros, killing 80, the worst ferry disaster in 35 years.

MAY 4–5, 2001 Pope John Paul II's visit is the first to this Christian Orthodox country by a Roman pontiff since 1054 and the first ever to Athens.

2002 Greece enters Eurozone.

2004 Greece soccer team wins European Championship; Olympic Games held in Athens.

2010 Greece suffers severe financial crisis; strikes and riots erupt in Athens and around the country.

Athenian **Architecture**

Athens has been continuously inhabited for some 7,000 years. Apart from ancient ruins that these days stake space alongside apartment blocks, you'll come upon Byzantine churches, 19th-century neoclassical buildings and parks, and a 21st-century cobblestone walkway on which to view them all.

Doric columns of Pentelic marble supporting the Parthenon.

Aegean Bronze Age (2800–1100 B.C.)

The Mideast concept of a building as a work of art can be seen in Mycenaean palaces, which featured colorful frescoes contrasted with massive stone blocks. For an idea of the style, see the Mycenaean artifacts at the **National Archaeological Museum.**

Hellenic Age (8th–5th C. B.C.)

All the principle temples and monuments of Athens were built in this period in the much-celebrated Doric order: Rectangular temples were made of limestone, tufa, and marble, with tapered columns and unadorned capitals. Beautiful, strong Mount Pendeli marble (called Pentelic marble) was used on the 447–438 B.C. **Parthenon,** a perfection of the style.

Late 5th C. B.C.

Doric elements are combined with a more restrained version of the Ionic order, recognized by their volute

Volute capitals fronting the Erechtheion.

(spiral-shape) capitals. The style can be seen in the **Erechtheion** and the **Temple of Athena Nike** on the Acropolis.

5th C. B.C.–2nd C. A.D.
Corinthian-order acanthus capitals come into vogue. These columns, such as those on the **Temple of Olympian Zeus,** feature a leaf design.

Early Christian Period (4th–7th C.)
Following Theodosius's ban of ancient cults in 437, Christianity takes root in Athens. The Christians did not build temples to the scale of ancient Greek monuments, rather constructing either cross-shaped domed churches or basilicas with sculpted capitals, cornices, and a screen separating the *naos* (church proper) from the sanctuary. Few early basilicas have survived, but there is a small-scale reconstruction of one at the **Byzantine and Christian Museum.**

Byzantine Period (8th–15th C.)
A great number of churches from the Byzantine period have survived in Athens. Typically, these are small, narrowly proportioned, domed, cross-shaped churches with inner frescoes and fine outer

The Byzantine Kapnikarea church, with its domed cathedral.

tile, brick masonry, and motifs, such as the **Kapnikarea.**

Post-Byzantine Period (16th–19th C.)
Architecture from this time is difficult to date, due to fragmentary remains of Frankish, Venetian, and Turkish monuments, which were constructed with a combination of older preexisting materials. The **Daphni monastery,** originally constructed in the 6th century, underwent many changes after Byzantine rule: Gothic pointed arches, for example, were added by Catholic monks.

Neoclassical Period (19th–20th C.)
Athens was an idyllic city of 200,000 by the end of the 19th century and was distinguished by a renewed

The neoclassical Academy of Athens, which emulates the Ionic Erechtheion.

interest in neoclassicism—a sentimental attachment to the indigenous ancient Greek traditions. Homes, courtyard gardens, and beautiful public buildings erected by wealthy Diaspora patrons all adhered to this style, epitomized by the **Academy of Athens,** the **University of Athens,** and the **National Library,** designed by the Hansen brothers. The 20th century marked a shift, though: The population reached 500,000 and new, modern multistoried office and apartment buildings went up, as was the fashion in other west European capitals. Greece was taking a cue from its installed German monarchy.

Interwar Period (1920s–1930s)

Athens grew to more than one million inhabitants in the 1930s, due to the relocation of Asia Minor refugees in 1919 to 1922 and migration from the countryside. The state turned a blind eye to illegal construction for much-needed housing. At the same time, British villas and garden suburbs in the north (in the **Psychiko** and **Filothei** neighborhoods) and south (in **Paleo Faliro**) sprouted up.

Postwar Period (20th C.)

With more rural migration the population continued to explode, and neighborhoods changed as property was sold to developers in exchange for one or more apartments in the building. An urban renewal project based on a 170-year-old plan to reclaim the chaotically overdeveloped and polluted city began in the 1990s, and the historic center was largely transformed to a pedestrian zone under the **Unification of the Archaeological Sites of Athens** plan, with restored and listed buildings and a pedestrian walkway connecting ancient sites.

Useful **Phrases & Menu Terms**

ENGLISH	GREEK	PRONUNCIATION
Hello/goodbye	Γειάσου Γειά σας	*Ya*-soo (singular, informal); *Ya*-sas (plural, singular polite)
Good morning	Καλημερα	Ka-li-*me*-ra
Good afternoon/ evening	Καλησπέρα	Ka-li-*spe*-ra
Goodnight (night)	Καληνύχτα	Ka-li-*nich*-ta (*nik*-ta)
Yes	Ναι	Nai
No	Οχι	*O*-hi
Please/you're welcome	Παρακαλω	Pa-ra-ka-*lo*
Thank you (very much)	Ευχαριστω (πολή)	Ef-ha-ri-*stow* (po-*lee*)
How are you?	Τι κάνετε?	Ti *ka*-ne-te?
Fine, thank you	Μιά χαρά, ευχαριστω	*Mya* ha-*ra*, ef-ha-ri-*stow*
Excuse me	Συγνωμη	Sig-*no*-mi
Sorry	Σόρι	*So*-ry
Give me . . .	Μου δωστε . . .	Mou *dhos*-te . . .
Do you speak English?	Μιλάτε αγγλικά?	Mi-la-te Angli-*ka*?

ENGLISH	GREEK	PRONUNCIATION
I understand	Καταλαβαίνω	Ka-ta-la-*ve*-no
I don't understand	Δεν καταλαβαίνω	Dhen ka-ta-la-*ve*-no
I know (it)	Το ξέρο	To *gze*-ro
Where is . . .	Που έιναι . . .	Pou ee-ne . . .
the station	Ο σταθμό	o stath-*mos*
a post office	Το ταχιδρομίο	to ta-chi-dhro-*mee*-o
a bank	Η τράπεζα	ee *tra*-pe-za
a hotel	Το ξενοδοχέιω	to xe-no-dho-*hee*-o
a restaurant	Το εστιατόριο	to estia-*tow*-ree-o
a pharmacy/chemist	Το φαρμακέιο	to farma-*kee*-o
the toilet	Η τουαλέτα	ee tooa-*le*-ta
a hospital	Το νοσοκομέιο	to no-so-ko-*mee*-o
Left	Αριστερά	A-ri-ste-*ra*
Right	Δεξιά	Dhex-*ya*
Straight	Ευθύα	Ef-*thee*-a
Tickets	Εισιτήρια	Ee-see-*tee*-ria
How much does it cost?	Πόσο κάνει?	*Po*-so *ka*-ni?
A one-way ticket	Ενα απλό εισιτήριο	*E*-na ap-*lo* is-i-*ti*-rio
A round-trip ticket	Ενα εισιτήριο με επιστροφη	*E*-na is-i-*ti*-rio me e-pi-*stro*-fi
Is there a discount for . . .	Ηπάρχει έ κπτωσι γιά . . .	Ee-*par*-hi ek-pto-si yia . . .
family	Οικογένεια	ee-ko-*gen*-ya
children	Παιδιά	pe-*dhia*
students	Φοιτητέ	fee-tee-*tes*
seniors	συνταξιούχο	syn-da-xi-*ou*-hos
What time is it?	Τη ωρα είναι?	Ti *o*-ra ee-ne?
When?	Πότε?	*Po*-teh?
When does (it) leave?	Πότε φεύγει?	*Po*-teh *fev*-gi?
This	Αυτό	Af-*tow*
Here	Εδω	Eh-*dho*
There	Εκεί	Eh-*key*

Numbers

One (1)	Ενα	*E*-na
Two (2)	Δύο	*Dhee*-o
Three (3)	Τρία	*Tree*-a
Four (4)	Τέσσερα	*Te*-se-ra
Five (5)	Πέντε	*Pen*-de
Six (6)	Έξι	*E*-xi
Seven (7)	Επτά	Ep-*ta*
Eight (8)	Οκτό	Ok-*to*
Nine (9)	Εννιά	En-*ya*
Ten (10)	Δέκα	*Dhe*-ka

ENGLISH	GREEK	PRONUNCIATION
Eleven (11)	Έντεκα	*En*-dhe-ka
Twelve (12)	Δώδεκα	*Tho*-dhe-ka
Thirteen (13)	Δεκατρία	Dhe-ka-*tree*-a
Fourteen (14)	Δεκατέσσερα	Dhe-ka-*te*-se-da
Fifteen (15)	Δεκαπέντε	Dhe-ka-*pen*-de
Sixteen (16)	Δεκα-έξι	Dhe-ka-*eh*-xi
Seventeen (17)	Δεκα-επτά	Dhe-ka ep-*ta*
Eighteen (18)	Δεκα-οχτω	Dhe-ka ok-*to*
Nineteen (19)	Δεκα-εννιά	Dhe-ka en-*ya*
Twenty (20)	Εικοσι	*Ee*-ko-see
Thirty (30)	Τριάντα	Tri-*an*-da
Forty (40)	Σαράντα	Sa-*ran*-da
Fifty (50)	Πενήντα	Pe-*nin*-da
One hundred (100)	Εκατό	Eh-ka-*to*

Menu Terms

Food	Φαγητό	Fa-gee-*to*
Water	Νερό	Neh-*ro*
Coffee	Καφέ	Ca-*feh*
Tea	Τσάι	*Tsa*-ee
A kilo/half-kilo	Ενα κιλό/Μισό κιλό	Ena kee-lo/mi-*so* kee-*lo*
of red/white wine	κόκκινο/άσπρο κρασί	*kok*-kino/*as*-pro kra-*see*
The bill please	Το λογαριασμό παρακαλω	To lo-ga-ri-az-*mo* pa-ra-ka-*lo*

Note: *Roll r so it sounds like a soft d. Dh sounds like the.*

Useful **Toll-Free Numbers & Websites**

Major International Airlines
AIR FRANCE
☎ *800/237-2747 (in U.S.)*
☎ *800/375-8723 (U.S. and Canada)*
☎ *087/0142-4343 (in U.K.)*
www.airfrance.com

ALITALIA
☎ *800/223-5730 (in U.S.)*
☎ *800/361-8336 (in Canada)*
☎ *087/0608-6003 (in U.K.)*
www.alitalia.com

BRITISH AIRWAYS
☎ *800/247-9297 (in U.S. and Canada)*
☎ *087/0850-9850 (in U.K.)*
www.british-airways.com

CHINA AIRLINES
☎ *800/227-5118 (in U.S.)*
☎ *022/715-1212 (in Taiwan)*
www.china-airlines.com

DELTA AIR LINES
☎ *800/221-1212 (in U.S. or Canada)*
☎ *084/5600-0950 (in U.K.)*
www.delta.com

EGYPTAIR
☎ 212/581-5600 (in U.S.)
☎ 020/7734-2343 (in U.K.)
☎ 09/007-0000 (in Egypt)
www.egyptair.com

EL AL AIRLINES
☎ 972/3977-1111 (outside Israel)
☎ *2250 (from any phone in Israel)
www.elal.co.il

EMIRATES AIRLINES
☎ 800/777-3999 (in U.S.)
☎ 087/0243-2222 (in U.K.)
www.emirates.com

IBERIA AIRLINES
☎ 800/722-4642 (in U.S. and Canada)
☎ 087/0609-0500 (in U.K.)
www.iberia.com

LUFTHANSA
☎ 800/399-5838 (in U.S.)
☎ 800/563-5954 (in Canada)
☎ 087/0837-7747 (in U.K.)
www.lufthansa.com

OLYMPIC AIRLINES
☎ 800/223-1226 (in U.S.)
☎ 514/878-9691 (in Canada)
☎ 087/0606-0460 (in U.K.)
www.olympicairlines.com

SWISS AIR
☎ 877/359-7947 (in U.S. and Canada)
☎ 084/5601-0956 (in U.K.)
www.swiss.com

TURKISH AIRLINES
☎ 90/212444-0-849
www.thy.com

US AIRWAYS
☎ 800/428-4322 (in U.S. and Canada)
☎ 084/5600-3300 (in U.K.)
www.usairways.com

Budget Airlines

AEGEAN AIRLINES
☎ 210/626-1000 (in U.S., Canada, and U.K.)
www.aegeanair.com

AIR BERLIN
☎ 087/1500-0737 (in U.K.)
☎ 018/0573-7800 (in Germany)
☎ 180/573-7800 (all others)
www.airberlin.com

EASYJET
☎ 870/600-0000 (in U.S.)
☎ 090/5560-7777 (in U.K.)
www.easyjet.com

Car-Rental Agencies

AUTO EUROPE
☎ 888/223-5555 (in U.S. and Canada)
☎ 0800/2235-5555 (in U.K.)
www.autoeurope.com

AVIS
☎ 800/331-1212 (in U.S. and Canada)
☎ 084/4581-8181 (in U.K.)
www.avis.com

BUDGET
☎ 800/527-0700 (in U.S.)
☎ 800/268-8900 (in Canada)
☎ 087/0156-5656 (in U.K.)
www.budget.com

DOLLAR
☎ 800/800-4000 (in U.S.)
☎ 800/848-8268 (in Canada)
☎ 080/8234-7524 (in U.K.)
www.dollar.com

HERTZ
☎ 800/645-3131
☎ 800/654-3001 (for international reservations)
www.hertz.com

THRIFTY
☎ 800/367-2277
☎ 918/669-2168 (international)
www.thrifty.com

Major Hotel Chains

BEST WESTERN INTERNATIONAL
☎ 800/780-7234 (in U.S. and Canada)
☎ 0800/393-130 (in U.K.)
www.bestwestern.com

DOUBLETREE HOTELS
☎ 800/222-TREE (800/222-8733) (in U.S. and Canada)
☎ 087/0590-9090 (in U.K.)
www.doubletree.com

HILTON HOTELS
☎ 800/HILTONS (800/445-8667) (in U.S. and Canada)
☎ 087/0590-9090 (in U.K.)
www.hilton.com

HOLIDAY INN
☎ *800/315-2621 (in U.S. and Canada)*
☎ *0800/405-060 (in U.K.)*
www.holidayinn.com

INTERCONTINENTAL HOTELS & RESORTS
☎ *800/424-6835 (in U.S. and Canada)*
☎ *0800/1800-1800 (in U.K.)*
www.ichotelsgroup.com

MARRIOTT
☎ *877/236-2427 (in U.S. and Canada)*
☎ *0800/221-222 (in U.K.)*
www.marriott.com

SHERATON HOTELS & RESORTS
☎ *800/325-3535 (in U.S.)*
☎ *800/543-4300 (in Canada)*
☎ *0800/3253-5353 (in U.K.)*
www.starwoodhotels.com/sheraton

WESTIN HOTELS & RESORTS
☎ *800/937-8461 (in U.S. and Canada)*
☎ *0800/3259-5959 (in U.K.)*
www.starwoodhotels.com/westin

Index

Index

See also Accommodations and Restaurant indexes, below.

Photo **Credits**

p i, left: © R. Ian Lloyd/Masterfile; p i, middle: © IML Image Group Ltd./Alamy Images; p i, right: © Stuart Dee/Getty Images; p ii: © Digital Vision/www.agefotostock.com; p ii: © P. Narayan/www.agefotostock.com; p ii: © Hemis/Alamy; p ii: © PCL/Alamy; p ii: © Georgios Makkas; p iii: © Courtesy King George Palace; p iii: © George Tsafos/Lonely Planet Images/Alamy Images; p iii: © Adrees Latif/Reuters/Corbis; p iii: © Courtesy Grande Bretagne; p iii: © Georgios Makkas; p vii: © Vergas/IML Image Group; p 4: © Alvaro Leiva/www.agefotostock.com; p 5: © Georgios Makkas; p 6 top: © Georgios Makkas; p 6 bottom: © Georgios Makkas; p 7: © Digital Vision/www.agefotostock.com; p 9: © Georgios Makkas; p 10 top: © ZeppeLine.gr; p 10 bottom: © Georgios Makkas; p 11: © Georgios Makkas; p 13 middle: © Benaki Museum, Athens, Greece/Gift of Irini Karakotsiou/The Bridgeman Art Library; p 13 bottom: © Georgios Makkas; p 14: © Alvaro Leiva/AGE Fotostock, Inc.; p 15: © Georgios Makkas; p 17: © Georgios Makkas; p 18 top: © Yannis Lefakis; p 18 bottom: © P. Narayan/www.agefotostock.com; p 19: © Georgios Makkas; p 20: © Alvaro Leiva/www.agefotostock.com; p 21: © P. Narayan/www.agefotostock.com; p 23: © Georgios Makkas; p 25 top: © Wolfgang Kaehler/Alamy Images; p 25 bottom: © Georgios Makkas; p 27: © George S de Blonsky/Alamy Images; p 28: © George Tsafos/Lonely Planet Images/AGE Fotostock, Inc.; p 31: © Georgios Makkas; p 32: © George Tsafos/Lonely Planet Images; p 33 top: © Franck Guiziou/AGE Fotostock, Inc.; p 33 bottom: © Georgios Makkas; p 34: © Georgios Makkas; p 37: © Yannis Lefakis; p 38 top: © Anders Blomqvist/Lonely Planet Images; p 38 bottom: © ZeppeLine.gr; p 41: © Yannis Lefakis; p 42 top: © Gianni Dagli Orti/Corbis; p 42 bottom: © Interfoto/Alamy Images; p 43 top: © IML Image Group Ltd./Alamy; p 43 bottom: © Anders Blomqvist/Lonely Planet Images; p 45: © Nils-Johan Norenlind/www.agefotostock.com; p 46: © Robert Harding Picture Library Ltd./Alamy; p 47: © ZeppeLine.gr; p 49: © JTB Photo Communications, Inc./Alamy; p 50 top: © ZeppeLine.gr; p 50 bottom: © ZeppeLine.gr; p 51: © Travel Ink/Nigel Bowen-Morris; p 53: © Spyros Bourboulis/AGE Fotostock, Inc.; p 54 top: © Patricia Fenn; p 54 bottom: © Georgios Makkas; p 55: © Hemis/Alamy; p 57: © Georgios Makkas; p 58: © Yannis Lefakis; p 59 top: © Georgios Makkas; p 59 bottom: © Georgios Makkas; p 61: © Kouri/IML/www.agefotostock.com; p 62 top: © Georgios Makkas; p 62 bottom: © ZeppeLine.gr; p 63: © Alan Benson/Lonely Planet Images; p 65 top: © David Sanger Photography/Alamy Images; p 65 bottom: © Jon Arnold Images/DanitaDelimont.com; p 67: © IML/SuperStock, Inc.; p 68 top: © Hristos Kissadjekian; p 68 bottom: © Velissarios Voutsas/IML Image Group; p 69: © PCL/Alamy; p 70: © Yannis Lefakis; p 73: © ZeppeLine.gr; p 74 top: © Yannis Lefakis; p 74 bottom: © ZeppeLine.gr; p 75: © ZeppeLine.gr; p 76 top: © ZeppeLine.gr; p 76 bottom: © ZeppeLine.gr; p 77 top: © Yannis Lefakis; p 77 bottom: © ZeppeLine.gr; p 78 top: © Ingolf Pompe 24/Alamy; p 78 bottom: © ZeppeLine.gr; p 79: © ZeppeLine.gr; p 80: © Georgios Makkas; p 81: © ZeppeLine.gr; p 82: © ZeppeLine.gr; p 83: © Georgios Makkas; p 85: © J.D. Dallet/www.agefotostock.com; p 86: © Georgios Makkas; p 87 top: © Georgios Makkas; p 87 bottom: © ZeppeLine.gr; p 89: © Imagestate/PhotoLibrary; p 90 bottom: © Sean Burke/Alamy Images; p 90 top: © Gianni Dagli Orti/The Art Archive/Alamy Images; p 91: © Russell Kord/Alamy Images; p 93 top: © TTL Images/Alamy Images; p 93 bottom: © Wilmar Photography/Alamy; p 95: © Yannis Lefakis; p 96: © Patrick Frilet/www.agefotostock.com; p 97: © Courtesy King George Palace; p 98: © George Atsametakis/IML Image Group; p 102 top: © Yannis Lefakis; p 102 bottom: © ZeppeLine.gr; p 103: © Yannis Lefakis; p 104: © ZeppeLine.gr; p 105: © Terry Harris Just Greece Photo Library/Alamy; p 106: © LOOK Die Bildagentur der Fotografen GmbH/Alamy; p 107 top: © ZeppeLine.gr; p 107 bottom: © Georgios Makkas; p 108: © ZeppeLine.gr; p 109: © George Tsafos/Lonely Planet Images/Alamy Images; p 110: © ZeppeLine.gr; p 114: © Terry Harris Just Greece PhotoLibrary/Alamy Images; p 115: © ZeppeLine.gr; p 116: © Terry Harris/Just Greece Photo Library/Alamy Images; p 117: © ZeppeLine.gr; p 118 top: © ZeppeLine.gr; p 118 bottom: © Courtesy King GeorgePalace; p 119: © Yannis Lefakis; p 120: © Yiorgos Ventouris/IML Image Group; p 121: © Adrees Latif/Reuters/Corbis; p 122: © Tom Daskalakis/IML Image Group; p 126: © Simela Pantzartzi/epa/Corbis; p 127: © Georgios Makkas; p 128: © Alex Rodopoulos/IML Image Group; p 129 top: © Alan King/Alamy; p 129 bottom: © Hristos Kissadjekian; p 131: © Half Note Jazz Club; p 132: © Georgios Makkas; p 133: © Courtesy Grande Bretagne; p 134: © Courtesy Athenaeum Intercontinental; p 138: © ZeppeLine.gr; p 139: © Courtesy Adrian Hotel; p 140: © Courtesy Athens Studio; p 141: © Courtesy Divani Palace; p 142 top: © Courtesy Electra Palace; p 142 bottom: © Travelstock44/Alamy; p 143 top: © Courtesy Grande Bretagne; p 143 bottom: © ZeppeLine.gr; p 145: © Courtesy King George Palace; p 146: © Courtesy O & B Hotel; p 147: © Georgios Makkas; p 149: © De Agostini/SuperStock, Inc.; p 151: © Yannis Lefakis; p 153 top: © Yannis Lefakis; p 153 bottom: © T. Papageorgiou/AGE Fotostock, Inc.; p 154: © Yannis Lefakis; p 157: © Georgios Makkas; p 158: © Georgios Makkas; p 159: © Loukas Hapsis/IML Image Group.

Notes